Acknowledgements

Without many precious people in my life, I would never have learned to hear God's whispering voice. Senators Elizabeth and Bob Dole, you were both role models and family to me in my twenties. Thank you both for the privilege of being part of your campaign and government staff over those formative years. Without you, I don't think I would have become a writer and conference speaker. Jennie Bower, you are a fabulous editor and this book is way better because of your hard work. Taylor Hanson, your creative skills for the design of the book inside and out were invaluable. Dr. Charles Kraft, you taught me about the Holy Spirit and let me be on your travelling prayer team in Africa and the United States. Walt Gerber, you mentored me in preaching and ministering to people at MPPC. Scott Dudley, you believed in my prophetic gift and encouraged me more than you know.

New Hope Peninsula Church family, thank you for the adventure of planting our church and for the honor of being your pastors for seven wonderful years. You were literally the hands and feet of Jesus to us during the years after Ben's bike wreck and Corey's horse accident. Dan and Pam Chun, you gave me a speaking platform at the Honolulu HIM and Life in the Spirit conferences, and you allowed me and my friends to minister to countless people in Hawaii. Sara Groves, Jordan Seng, Jack Deere, Judith MacNutt, Daniel Brown, Alissa Picker, and Patti Pierce: All of you truly have "big ears" that hear God's voice, and I've learned tons listening to you. Lisa, Kim, Jane, Julie, Sharon, Cynthia, Kathleen, and Bill: It has been a joy to partner with you in Eagles Nest, helping people learn to pray for healing, to intercede, and to hear God's voice. My Hawaiian Christian family, Julie, Vince, Stefanie, Ross, Laura, Jason, and so many of you who have embraced me while speaking on Oahu: You have taught me what real prayer warriors look like. Cindy and Billy Schwaab: thank you for your precious friendship and encouragement, especially in the Stanford ER the night Ben was hit.

Thank you, Mom and Dad, for being amazing people of God who taught me what it means to walk through life's fires holding onto Jesus. My sister, Amy: You are one of the strongest people I know, who despite a snake bite, a lightning strike, and a flash flood, managed to hang onto Jesus and embrace joy in hardship. My brothers, Brian and Stephen: You make me laugh out loud, and you're not just my brothers, you are my friends.

Corey, Annie, and Benji, my amazing kids, you all teach me way more about hearing God's voice than I'll ever be able to teach you. I love you with all my heart. Finally, my husband, Ben, my hero and love of my life. Thank you for bearing with me in love and being my greatest cheerleader.

It's impossible to list all of you friends who have loved and supported me in my journey to tell people about the God who whispers, so forgive me if I forgot to mention your name. You know who you are. Huge thanks for being there for me.

Most importantly, thank you, Father, Son, and Holy Spirit, that You are the God who whispers. Words can't express my humble gratitude for teaching me how to hear Your whispering voice and for allowing me to encourage others that they can hear you whisper too.

GOD IS WHISPERING TO YOU

CHRISTY PIERCE

ISBN: 1492975036

ISBN-13: 978-1492975038

FOR BEN, COREY, ANNIE, AND BENJI

My greatest joy in life, after following Jesus, is being the mom in our family. Each of you have taught me way more about how God whispers than I could ever teach you. I love you with all my heart.

Contents

God's Special Kid

Dear God, are you really invisible, or is that a trick?
Lucy, *Children's Letters to God*

*No eye has seen, no ear has heard, no mind has conceived
what God has prepared for those who love him.*
1 Corinthians 2:9 [1]

Some moments in life are written on our hearts with permanent, unfading ink. One of those days for me was when my daughter, Corey, was four years old, and I heard her singing in the backyard. Standing at the kitchen sink washing the dinner dishes, I heard her little voice drifting through the kitchen window singing this sweet little song,

"God I love the birds! I love the bees! I love the sky, but you tell me the truth: You love me!"

Something about that simple, beautiful song drew me, so I put down the kitchen towel and went outside into the yard. Corey was completely unaware of my presence, and she kept joyfully dancing and singing, so I just watched her. Finally, I got her attention and asked,

"Corey, honey, that song is just beautiful! Did you learn that at church?"

---

[1] All Scripture references are from the New International Version of the
Holy Bible (NIV) unless otherwise specified herein.

She turned to me and said in a matter-of-fact voice something I will never forget,

"Oh no, Mommy. I didn't learn that at church. Nobody taught it to me. It's a special song that Jesus just put into my heart." She paused, looked up at the sky, and said, "I think it's because I'm God's special kid." That moment is forever etched in my soul because I knew that the Spirit of God had, in some very real way, gotten through to a four-year-old little girl the truth: She was God's special kid.

That day, I was not only grateful to God that He spoke to my daughter this beautiful message of truth, I was also a little jealous. I kept thinking, *God, my whole life would be different if I understood that I was your special kid! Help me to get that truth inside of me!*

How would your life be different if you understood, not just in your head, but deep in your soul, that you are God's special kid? How would things change in your life if you prayed to God and actually heard Him speaking back to you in such a way that you just knew it was God whispering directly to you?

You and I live in a noisy world of ringing cell phones, beeping text messages, e-mails, tweets, Instagrams, and all kinds of other voices screaming for our attention. Every day, morning until night, people are all around us talking, talking, talking. Most of us are pulled in so many different directions that some days we can barely hear our own voice, much less tune into God's quiet, whispered one. Could He not just send us an e-mail? Or would it not at least be simpler to communicate to the Living God through a picture on Instagram, like we do with everyone else?

Of course, we all know that God's communication with us does not usually involve the normative ways of sending and receiving messages in today's world. And yet, God is talking to you all the time! God is constantly trying to get through how much He loves you and cares about the things that you are worried about right now.

The God who whispers does not have favorites. You are being invited, personally, to draw closer to Him and to learn to hear His voice. Not everyone understands this invitation. Not everyone responds. Only God really knows the deep desires of your heart. Remember, He made you. He knows the language of your heart and how to get through to you. God longs to talk to you in new ways that touch the deep parts of your soul so that you might surprise yourself by saying, "WOW, God is speaking to me! I never knew that He loved me that much!"

This is a different kind of book. There are a lot of good books that will teach you about the theology of how God whispers. But as you read this book, my hope is that your faith will grow as you hear many stories of God speaking to ordinary people in extraordinary ways. I pray that you learn the different ways God has whispered to people from biblical times until today. I am hoping you are inspired to open yourself up to new ways of hearing God's voice more clearly.

I am convinced God wants more for you. I pray that as you read this book, God will help you actually experience His whispering voice speaking to you directly about what matters to you. Not only that, my hope is that this book is a turning point in your relationship with God, where you start to hear Him talking more in your daily life.

Yes, I get it. I understand completely that this may sound like a bold, wild, magical kind of prayer that might even seem impossible to some of you. I mean, come on! How can I even pray that kind of prayer without knowing you and your story, right? Good point. I can only respond by saying this: I do not know you, but I do know the God who is whispering to you, trying to get your attention all the time. God loves you and longs to gently speak to you about the things that are heavy on your heart.

For over 20 years, I have seen God whisper to people who thought that God speaks to everyone else but them. For decades, I have seen God break through the hardest, most skeptical hearts with whispers from His heart to theirs that blow them away.

What could be more important than hearing God? Think about it. Nothing has the power to change your life, to rock your world, to pull you out of the pit, to give you hope more than the God of the Universe saying to you, *I see you. I know all that you are facing. I am here, and I will help you.*

This book is for those of you who are tired of all the noise. It is for the hungry, the wounded, for those who want more of Jesus. It is for those of you who have heard about, studied about, or even preached about the "abundant life" Jesus spoke of, but still feel lacking in your own personal experience of hearing God speak. It is also for those intellectual followers of Jesus who may know a lot about Jesus and the Bible, but have always hoped to experience God communicating more on a personal level. It is for those of you who have been disappointed, who feel that God speaks to everyone else but you. Believe me when I tell you this: I am the most ordinary, broken person you will ever meet. Trust me. If I can hear God whisper, you can. If you do not have a relationship with God yet, please do not simply disqualify yourself. The God of the Universe knows your name and is especially inviting you to hear His voice in a life-changing way.

You might also have some "what if" questions when it comes to actually hearing God whisper. Good! I have heard hundreds of "what if" questions and fears when it comes to God speaking including, "What if I hear God wrong?" "What if I turn into one of those weirdos shrieking, 'I heeeeaaar the Lord saying buy a rooster and name him Jim'?" "What if God tells me to move to Africa?" "What if God reads all my dirty mail and tells everyone else?" "What if I try hearing God for myself, but end up disappointed?"

I will address these questions and more when it comes to hearing God speak. No one needs to become a pariah or act like someone they are not in order to hear God whisper. God knows you, and He knows the exact way to whisper into your life above the noise in a way you will be able to hear. As you read, my hope is that *you will actually experience God whisper in new ways that build your faith and intimacy with God*. Consequently, you will find practical exercises at the end of each chapter called, "God, please whisper to me now." These exercises are designed for you individually, or in a small group setting, to help you to experience God whispering to you more in your life.

Despite all excess noise screaming for your attention, God is reaching out to you. Jesus is extending a very personal invitation with your very name on it. God has encouraging things to say that will build you up. He knows all about the things waking you in the middle of the night. He knows about all your dreams and fears. Only God knows the exact words you need to hear that will breathe hope into your weary soul. The truth is, God is whispering to you! You can hear God for yourself. You really can. May this book be the beginning of a new chapter in your spiritual life, a holy adventure, where you learn to hear God's voice in ways you never dreamed possible.

Dare to believe! His promise is the same now as it was in the words of the New Testament, "Now to Him, who is able to do immeasurably more than all we ask or imagine, according to His power that is at work within us" (Ephesians 3:20).

You Can Hear God And Not Be Weird

Call to me and I will answer you and tell you great and unsearchable things you do not know.
Jeremiah 33:3

Your inadequacy is your first qualification.
John Gaynor Banks, *The Master and the Disciple*

You do not need a Ph.D. to hear God. You do not need special gifts or talents. God loves speaking to normal and ordinary people. I am someone who values being very real, and this book has some very vulnerable and personal stories to prove that. When you see what an imperfect, messy person I can be, I think you will be encouraged.

If you have ever thought, *I can't hear God because I'm too sinful, broken, or faithless*, you are wrong. I am probably the most broken, ordinary person on the planet. Some days, I am more faithless than faith-filled. If God speaks to me and I can hear Him, I promise you this: You can hear God's voice too.

As a mom of three young children, I can hardly hear my own voice most days. In fact, sometimes I feel like I am just trying to make it until five o'clock. After that, I find myself wondering, *What time is it legal to send kids to bed and go to bed yourself?!* If you need proof that I am a normal person who is far from perfect, I could tell you tons of stories.

As I write, one funny (and embarrassing) story comes to mind, which will give you a window into the reality of my ordinary-ness. It was a sunny morning in the San Francisco Bay area where I live. A typical morning where I am shouting before school,

"Hurry up you guys! Corey do you have your backpack?! Annie it's P.E. day, don't forget your tennis shoes! Benji, for the millionth time, brush your teeth!!" So, I was a little more irritable than normal, but I had a good reason. It was my turn to drive for the San Francisco Bay Wetlands field trip. Ugh!

You have to understand, I am not a morning person. That fact is especially true when I am driving 45 minutes to a field trip with kids yelling in the back seat. Hence, it is time for an emergency trip to Starbucks! When I got to the counter, I said to the barista,

"I'll have the biggest, most caffeine-filled thing you've got!" She did not even crack a smile. (She, apparently, wasn't a morning person either!) Guzzling my Starbucks *Venti Triple Latte*, off we go to the wetlands. Honestly, I was a little scared (but not because there were four boys throwing Goldfish crackers in the back seat as I maneuvered the stop-and-go of the backed up traffic on the 101 with tiny orange fish whizzing past my peripheral). The truth? I was afraid I might screw up my job as parent volunteer at the wetlands.

Do I sound paranoid? Maybe. But you have to understand this was not just any field trip. You see, if you want to chaperon the infamous wetlands field trip, you need a Ph.D. in ecological studies. Not really, but they are serious as a heart attack that you had better be familiar with the wetlands rules! There are several required preparation meetings where they instruct you how to enforce "trash-less" lunches for each kid and how to ensure no young troublemaker decides to use the wetland as his or her own trash bin for used gum.

If one wild boy decides to run after a Blue Heron and torment it, you are held responsible. Oh my, the pressure is enough to turn my stomach as I write about it. But, I was pretty sure I was ready. I had studied and prepared. I had my trash-less lunch. Most importantly, I had downed my Starbucks.

I felt thoroughly prepared for a great day at the wetlands. The first half of the day went fine. We saw the wildlife. Each kid was accounted for, and no child threw rocks at the waterfowl.

After lunch, we went across the long bridge out into the wetlands with the tour guide. Our little group of 20 children and four parents admired the natural beauty of marsh grasses teeming with wildlife as we walked peacefully out on the bridge over the marshes. It was really beautiful, and I was surprised that it was actually peaceful, even with all those potential trash-throwers around.

Then, reality broke through that moment of peace as my cell phone started buzzing. Quietly and secretly, I pulled the phone out of my pocket and saw a familiar area code number. It was Dan Chun, my friend and president of Hawaiian Islands Ministries. *Darn!* I thought. I was speaking at their conference, and this was the third call I had missed. Glancing at the naturalist who was speaking to the children about 50 feet ahead of me, I stopped and quickly answered the phone.

"Hi Dan," I whispered, hunkering down to the level of the 2nd grade heads in front of me. "I can't talk long because I'm out on a bridge in the Wetlands…" Before I could say much more, a creature from the wetlands ferociously attacked me! A very large, black and yellow bee dive-bombed my head.

Let me take this moment to say: I hate bees. I started waving my hands and shrieking, swatting it away. Before I knew which end was up, my cell phone flew from my hand and landed just over the bridge, right in the middle of the wetlands.

I froze. I was in shock. I looked ahead guiltily at the speaker and children, and miraculously they were turned the other way. They had not witnessed the atrocious act of my metallic cell phone with its non-recycled lithium-ion battery flying into the precious, protected-by-armed-guards marsh habitat.

I ran to the edge of the bridge, frantically saying to myself, *Breathe deep. Be calm. Christy, surely you can get it with a stick or something?* As I looked for my phone over the edge of the bridge, I realized to my utter horror that my cell phone is laying face up in the marsh mud, with Dan's raised voice saying,

"Christy? Are you there? Christy, are you there?" I swear to you that my heart stopped beating. The children swarmed to the edge of the pathway. One kid yelled,

"HEY! EVERYONE COME LOOK! OVER HERE! SOME IDIOT HAS THROWN A CELLPHONE INTO THE WETLANDS." At that pronouncement, all 20 children and the naturalist ran to the side of the bridge. I am sweating by now, thinking to myself, *Be cool. Who says it has to be my cell phone that is now resting comfortably on the delicate foliage of a protected marsh?* But, no. Dan has to keep shouting,

"Christy are you there? Christy, we have a bad connection talk louder." It is over. The entire group looks at me, as if on cue, and I see 50 pairs of wide, judging eyes looking right at me. The naturalist had a very unnatural look of horror on her face. At that point, I pondered jumping over the bridge myself.

I tried to explain that there was a large killer bee on the loose that was responsible. No one believed me. The kids were laughing hysterically, but for some odd reason, the naturalist did not partake in the hilarity. She called the Wetlands Director, who had to come out, clad in wading boots, to valiantly walk out through the marsh and retrieve it. Anxiously, we all watched and she made the declaration,

"TOO LATE!" The tide came rolling in, and we watched as a Blue Heron maneuvered around my phone. Thankfully, Dan had finally hung up and was no longer yelling my name. Still, it was sad and embarrassing to see these majestic, protected birds step around an iPhone 4 with a pink polka dot cover amidst the untouched marsh grasses. Not to mention, my kid's faces were the screen saver.

Unfortunately, my desecration of the wetlands sage did not die quickly. Two years later, my daughter graduated from White Oaks Elementary school. At her graduation, each fourth grader was allowed to stand up and say their favorite memory in the past five years of school. The principal called on the first student and she said, (You guessed it...),

"My favorite part was when Mrs. Pierce threw her cellphone into the Wetlands." Great! I was hopeful we had moved on, but after listening to all 110 fourth graders share their favorite memories and 75 list my cell phone incident as their top favorite memory, I realized I would never live down the title, "Wetland Desecration Mom."

In fact, even though we have all come to laugh about it, you should know that I am still not allowed at the wetlands. This is a rule strictly enforced by my children—and the school. In fact, my husband had to drive Annie and Benji on their wetlands field trip. For some strange reason, they did not want their mom there? Go figure. I am told that the naturalist now always mentions before each trip begins,

"Parents, please put your cell phones away, and do not get them out. One parent threw hers in the Bay and it is still there today."

Well, it has been four years since my cell phone saga in the wetlands, and despite the lessons learned, I am still the same imperfect, broken person. I am an ordinary mom who has good days, and as you can see, some not-so-good days.   Some days, I am full of faith. Other days, I feel faithless. Through it all, I have learned that God still wants to speak in amazing ways to people who want to hear His voice. It is true. It can happen for you.

Hearing God's voice has been a life-long journey. As I speak on this topic in various parts of the country, I have found that people have very different impressions of what hearing God means. If you could take requests, most folks would vote "yes" to a more intimate connection with God where they could actually hear His voice in their lives. Most people would say they would like God's direction and counsel as they are making big decisions or trying to parent their kids better.

Sleepless nights, anxious days, and painful relationships push us to the breaking point where we some days wonder, *Is God really listening? Is God even there?* We may intellectually believe that God loves us. But we want more: We want to believe that God cares enough to communicate with us about our worries and dreams.

I consistently hear a common concern from people when it comes to hearing God. Many people come to me and privately confess their personal worries. They will pull me aside and say something like,

"Christy, I really do want to hear God speak, but I don't want to turn into one of those weird people you see on TV shouting, 'I heeeeeaaar the Loooorrrd saying to me you quit your job, move to the rain forest, and study green tree snakes.'" Others will tell me that they have had people say to them,

"God told me to tell you that you screwed up this or that in your life." People do not want to be labeled as wacky. They also do not want to be read to from Isaiah's prophetic, judgmental scroll. They just want to hear God in a way that makes sense to them.

Yes, I am just an ordinary person (especially in the wetlands, where I become some sort of derelict). Over time, God has graciously taught me that He is indeed the Living God, who is alive and loves to whisper to His kids. He has been whispering to me for some time now. He is whispering to you too.

Not only that, but God can package His whispering voice in the very unique way that you need in order to hear Him. You do not have to be weird to hear God. You do not have to be someone else. You can be you—flaws and all—and hear God whisper. What would that look like for your life?

GOD, PLEASE WHISPER TO ME NOW...

Do you believe God would really whisper to you directly?

Do you have a picture in mind of the kind of people God talks to in life? What does that picture look like?

Do you truly believe you are God's special kid?

2

Just Be Yourself

Before I formed you in the womb, I knew you.
Jeremiah 1:5

What I thought I wanted, and what I got instead,
leaves me broken, yet somehow peaceful.
Sara Groves, "What I Thought I Wanted"

I grew up in Kansas City in a very loving family. I cannot imagine having parents who loved me more. As the first grandchild with many adoring grandparents, aunts, and uncles, I was loved from an early age. But, as you have probably experienced yourself, life can be harsh. For my family, a very traumatic event would change the course of our lives forever. When I was just five years old, my six-month-old brother died of Sudden Infant Death Syndrome (SIDS). I do not remember much at that point in life, but I do remember sadness. And fear.

Understandably, my parents were devastated by this loss. Losing a baby is something few people can fathom. It is one of the most horrible, difficult things any parent could ever face and my parents are truly heroes to me.

I will never know how they picked up and managed to raise a family of four children to love God and to love one another after that loss. Although my mom and dad were crushed by this heartbreak, they clung to God and to one another. Thanks to God's grace and their commitment to us, we were sheltered from much of the trauma. Yes, there was lots of love in my childhood, but no family escapes such a traumatic event without suffering in some capacity.

Trauma like that for a small child is often blocked out for years. Consequently, I do not remember much about life as a young child. What I do know is that a deep sadness entered my heart. The worst part was the fear, which began to torment my mind as a child whispered scary messages like, *Look out! You never know when something bad is going to happen.* That anxiety stayed with me way into my adult life.

Although I became a Christian as a teenager, I still struggled with ongoing anxiety and depression. In fact, I began running away from God in high school. I tried many things to numb the pain that was deep inside. Drinking, dating, achieving, and performing were all masks I hid behind. At the University of Kansas, I was Vice President of my sorority, an honor student, and on my way to law school. On the surface, my life looked like a picture of success. Inside, it was a vastly different story.

I ended up in Washington, D.C. working for the secretary of transportation, Elizabeth Dole. At 23, I became one of the youngest in the inner-circle of the "Dole for President" campaign. Bob and Elizabeth Dole became mentors and surrogate parents to me. They were people of extraordinary character, honesty, and were truly working to make the world a better place. On the presidential campaign, I was responsible for overseeing all the advance teams and scheduling for Mrs. Dole. My job required travel with the Presidential entourage—and travel we did. Some days we flew to four cities a day.

It was a fast-paced life of 15-hour days, travelling to three cities in a day, and running in national media and Washingtonian power circles. There is something about the adrenaline rush of Air Force One, press conferences, and cheering crowds that is extremely addictive. People can be intoxicated by the power and glamour of the lifestyle, and it was certainly exciting for me. I loved Senator and Elizabeth Dole, and I loved my job.

But no one saw the real me. I became exhausted from seven-day work weeks and sleepless nights. I weighed about 100 pounds no matter what I ate. One day, sitting at my downtown Washington, D.C. office, I called my brother, Brian (one of the funniest people I know), to vent about my private burnout. I remember whispering to him on the phone, searching for words to describe the crazy-busy life I was trying to survive.

"Bri, I've got some big problems," I began. "Everyday, I'm crossing the street to a deli and buying a whole chicken. Then I come back to my desk, return calls to reporters, and I while I'm on the phone, I eat the whole chicken! It's embarrassing, Brian! Sometimes people will come in and see chicken bones on my desk!" I continued breathlessly, "Then, I go home and order a pizza for dinner, and eat the whole thing! I can't understand why I still only weigh 100 pounds." My brother listened quietly and then replied,

"Wow, Chris. That's 27 chickens a month."

Brian had nailed it. I was wasting away under all the pressure and stress. Despite the glamour of my *West Wing* life, my prayer life consisted of one word: "HELP!" as I crawled into the shower at the end of each day. I remember thinking, *There must be more to life, must be more to faith in God than I'm experiencing!*

On Sundays, I turned off my beeper and went to church for an hour. Other days, I listened to sermons. I tried to read the Bible between pouring over the next day's campaign schedule on each flight I took. I vividly remember begging God to show up and to speak to me. In my head I believed that God loved me. In my heart, however, I felt a million miles away from any real experience of Jesus or His love.

The day the campaign ended, we were in a blizzard in Illinois. When we found out that Bush had won, everyone was in shock, not wanting to accept the reality that the "Dole for President" campaign was over for good. Secretly, I was relieved.

Do not misunderstand me: I loved the Doles and my friends on the campaign. We were like family. I desperately wanted them to win, and I worked myself to the point of exhaustion trying to help that dream become a reality. And yet, something inside me was afraid that if we made it to the White House, I would be dead!

Standing in front of the television, watching the campaign results pour in, my response was quiet relief, *Oh well, I guess we have to get out our resumes!* The next day I flew home to Kansas City with visions of rest and chicken noodle soup.

When I got home, my visions of rest and healing were shattered. Remember the Bible verse where God says, "For my thoughts are not your thoughts, neither are your ways my ways" from Isaiah 55:8? I was about to learn that life lesson, firsthand. While I had visions of peace and chicken noodle soup, God had another plan that would mean deep healing through the fire of suffering.

When I arrived in Kansas City, I went from the frying pan straight into the fire. My family, who had valiantly held it together for 20 years after our own tragedy, was now in a major meltdown. Long story short: We went from a family of affluence to wondering how to buy food for tomorrow and how to keep the water and lights on.

In the midst of this financial crisis, my sister, Amy, was bitten on the heel by a Copperhead snake. In excruciating pain, she was rushed to the Emergency Room to be treated for the snakebite. When the E.R. doctor heard what happened, he said,

"Amy, did you bring the snake with you?" She stared at him in unbelief. *Oh yeah, a big Copperhead snake just bit my heel, and I thought I'd see if I could catch him and keep it for a pet!* Hardly. The doctor was not all that crazy, though, because apparently if a snake has a bacterial infection, the hospital can run tests on the snake itself in order to find the best treatment for the patient.

They did not treat her with the anti-venom, and we discovered the hard way that Amy was not only bitten by a Copperhead snake, but a sick, bacteria-ridden snake carrying an infection that attacked Amy's body one organ at a time. That year Amy almost died several times, and we rushed over and over again to the hospital as she fought multiple infections.

Could it get worse? Yes. My sister, who is this amazing woman of God, managed to overcome this pain and become a local anchorperson for *Good Morning America*. One morning, as the early morning news reporter, Amy got up at five a.m. in the middle of a big thunderstorm. If you are not from the Midwest, you might not realize that thunderstorms are pretty darn scary. She drove through the torrential thunder and lightning and arrived soaking wet at the radio station. Amy was just in time to get into the sound booth and make the morning news. She put on the headphones and began,

"Good Morning! It's six a.m. I'm Amy Varney, and here's the news…" Suddenly, a huge crashing sound rattled the radio station and everything shook like an earthquake. Amy screamed in pain as she felt an electric jolt hit her body. To her horror, she realized she had actually been struck by lightning. She ripped off the headset as her colleague ran in shouting,

"Amy! Amy! Are you OK? Oh goodness, your face!" The earphones had acted like a lightning rod, burning her head where they had been touching her skin. The padding on the earphones had literally saved her life. Later, the firemen who examined the site said that lightning had struck the top of the radio tower, and the electricity poured down the structure. It then went into the radio monitor and zapped poor Amy since she was hooked up to the soundboard.

Bitten by a snake. Struck by lightning. Come on! How much can one person take? My Midwestern dry-humored brothers were teasing her after it all and said,

"Well, Aim, you're still good for some things—like jump-starting a car!" We had to laugh or we would cry. One thing was sure, we were pretty ordinary people, but we were facing extraordinary things. It seemed like we had a dark cloud over us and an enemy against us.

The good news was that God had our attention. Even people who were not Christians felt there was some sort of "enemy" against our family. The strange, yet wonderful, thing was that God was powerfully using all of this to create hearts that would seek Him as never before. It was in this fire of suffering that I truly learned to hear God's voice. We were so desperate for God that we were on our knees constantly. For the first time, I understood Paul's words, "Pray without ceasing" because we had no choice.

We went to every prayer meeting we could find. At that time, my sister and I joined a small prayer group that would forever change our lives. Each week we showed up and asked people to pray for us. Looking back, this group was the start of my journey in hearing God's voice.

We would pray for God's whispers in the midst of pain. In our inadequacy, God was faithful. He showed up. He began to whisper. He began to heal. He drew us into a deeper intimacy than any of us had ever known in our Christian lives. Turns out, this group was connected with the School of World Mission at Fuller Theological Seminary.

The School of World Mission invited me to go to Kenya to be part of a prayer team ministry to missionaries. I had no idea what I was doing. Me, pray? I was just an ordinary, broken person who needed prayer myself. But I went along for the ride, and Africa changed my life forever. This Washingtonian skeptic saw people healed and began to hear God in ways I never dreamed possible.

Chuck Kraft, a professor at Fuller Theological Seminary's School of World Mission, was the speaker and leader of the trip, which was to train missionaries all over Kenya about hearing God, healing, and spiritual warfare. Chuck is an amazing man of God who teaches people how to pray for healing, spiritual warfare and stuff like that.

Frankly, I was just hoping to have some of these big prayer warriors pray for me, but as God humorously arranged it, I was going along as a prayer minister. At the conference, two missionaries invited us to come visit their ministry to the Maasai tribe in the heart of the Rift Valley. It was a wild adventure few people ever get to experience, and though I did not know it yet, my Washingtonian worldview of God was about to be shattered.

Our trip was essentially meant to encourage and support a missionary family who had been serving there for 12 years. Twelve years, I might add, where only a handle full of the tribesmen had come to know Jesus and where daily life was literally an African safari of poisonous snakes, unsafe drinking water, and illness. Their unswerving faith and devotion to their call to this field was daunting.

Here I was, fresh off the break-neck campaign trail, trying to follow Jesus in the ups and downs of my life in Kansas City, and suddenly these giants of the faith were looking to us to bring a prayer and healing ministry to an unbelieving village.

Considering the majority of my prayer life had consisted of the words "God, help!" I felt a little out of my league as the team headed to the Maasai village to do healing prayer ministry. One of the two Christians in the village asked us to visit his hut because his wife was sick. He announced to the whole village that the "Christian healing prayer experts from the United States" were going to pray for her.

I stared at his eager face and into the eyes of those dear missionaries, and I thought to myself, *Great. We are going to pray. Nothing is going to hap-*

pen. *And then the few Christians in the village are going to give up on following Jesus.* It is safe to say that my faith was at an all-time low. We crawled into their dusty hut on our hands and knees in order to see his wife. She was curled up in a ball on the floor and looked like she was dying. Later, we learned she had Tuberculosis and had been sick with fever and lung problems for months. The man asked us to pray for her; my stomach was in knots. We prayed a few simple prayers, asking God for a miracle of healing. Amen.

We crawled out of the hut and stood up. I was prepared to continue on, obviously not expecting what happened next: She got up. And she got up to serve us tea, smiling.

We had a big problem. Most of the village was now excitedly shouting, and everyone began to line up for healing prayer. One after one, we prayed for these Maasai people, and I saw miracles I did not think happened anymore. People with crippled legs were healed. People with eye problems could now see. One by one, we prayed, and many people were healed that day.

Now, if I had not seen this with my own eyes, I never would have believed it could happen. In fact, I kept telling the brave Maasai man, the lone Christian who had faith that his wife could be healed, that I was blown away by God's healing and in complete shock at what was happening before my very eyes. He looked at me and said in an excited, yet humble voice,

"I don't know why you are so surprised? It says right here in your Bible that you will lay hands on the sick, pray, and they will be healed." I stared at the man and said,

"My friend, I am a Washingtonian skeptic. Things like this just don't happen in my world!" My little box I had put God in was falling apart.

Even more amazing was a letter we received two weeks later. I opened the letter from those two missionaries to the Maasai, which I thought would be a nice thank you note or something. Instead, it was another story straight out of the book of Acts. Apparently, a week after we left, a Maasai warrior was out in the bush and was bitten by a black mamba snake, whose bite can kill in less than two hours.

The missionaries, however, reported that some people went to the man and prayed for healing right there in the bush. Everyone was astonished when the man showed up at church that afternoon completely healed! Soon, the whole village was celebrating. Later, the missionaries went with a huge crowd from the village and they baptized believers in the river.

This was the kind of stuff that happens in the Bible. I just did not believe it could happen today—and if I did, I would need to see it with my very eyes. And then suddenly, I was seeing and experiencing things that I never dreamed possible in my Christian journey.

In fact, I went back to Kansas City shaking my head. One thing was for sure: God definitely had my full attention now. I was listening more closely. I now expected Him to speak in new ways. All this stuff made me want to learn more, and I packed my bags ready to head to Pasadena, California to attend seminary. I was all ready to go when I got an unexpected phone call from Elizabeth Dole.

"Christy?" her voice on the other line rang out. "I just got appointed Secretary of Labor. Would you come back and help out? I would like you to join my staff." I was touched and honored. Still, everything in me was screaming, *I do NOT want to go back to Washington and the days of 27 chickens!* So I told Elizabeth in the nicest way I knew how,

"Thank you so much, but I've had some pretty amazing God-experiences and I'm heading to Fuller Seminary to be a pastor." After all, my life had changed dramatically. I had seen suffering. I had seen miraculous healing. Surely that meant I had a new call, right? The thought of going back to Washington, D.C. felt like going back to another planet. But Elizabeth said very plainly,

"Well, Christy, you better pray about it because God might just be calling you here." Darn. She was right; so I did. As I prayed with my small group, God spoke to us through some very clear words and visions, and we all sensed God wanted me to go back to D.C. So I gave up my dream of going to seminary and went reluctantly back to the life of 27 chickens.

This chapter of my life I call, "Washington: Book Two." My time as a Special Assistant to the Secretary of Labor Elizabeth Dole was very different this time. It was the same Washington, D.C. with press conferences, White House briefings, crazy travel schedules, and some nasty political people.

Yes, the Washington, D.C. political world was the same. But this time, I was different. When I first arrived, I have to admit I had these grandiose ideas of what God might do through me since I had experienced God's presence and power in extraordinary ways since the presidential campaign. After all I had seen, surely God was calling me back to do the same extraordinary things there, right? I do not know what I expected. Maybe I secretly had visions of people being healed at press conferences. Perhaps I thought I would see demons cast out of the national media. What I do know is that, once again, God works in mysterious ways that we do not expect. My first morning back at work will always be a special memory.

It was 7:30 a.m., and I was driving my car past the Lincoln Memorial on my way to my office near Capitol Hill. Listening to some worship music in my car, I pulled into the parking garage. I showed the security guard my pass and jumped into the elevator. I prayed, *Lord, use me today to impact people powerfully here in the Labor Department. Amen.* Before the elevator doors opened, I heard God's quiet whisper, *Christy, I've called you here to love these people.* I was stunned. What? Surely, I had heard wrong. I started talking to God, trying to make my point in case He did not already know the grandiose dreams of my heart: *But Lord, some of these staff members are pretty cut-throat. They're competitive! Jesus, I don't even really like these people! How am I supposed to love them?*

But God was serious. He kept whispering to me over and over again. I knew that I was powerless to do this in my own strength. So, everyday, I tried my best, and climbed into that elevator praying, *Jesus, give me your eyes to see these people like you do. Help me to love them and be humble.* Each day, God gave me His love for these people.

Pretty soon, I became known as "Christy, the gal with connections to the Big Guy in the Sky." Very often, staff members would come undercover, as if looking over their shoulders to see if anyone saw them, to my office asking for prayer. God began to touch people. Some came to faith in Christ. The Lord would give me pictures or impressions as I prayed for people that only God could have known would touch them daily, I was astounded by God's deep love for these people and humbled that He would use me to show His compassion to these friends. You heard me right: these friends.

My friends at the state department held a weekly Bible study. One of them heard me describe my story in Africa and invited me to speak before the Bible study one evening. I naively said,

"Sure, but I'm not a theologian or a Bible expert. I'm just an ordinary person. But if you want, I'll come and share what I've seen." The night before I was supposed to speak, I had one of the first clear experiences of God whispering to me in an unusual way. At 2 a.m., I woke up hearing a quiet whisper in my mind saying over and over again: *Ezekiel 2:4. Ezekiel 2:4. Ezekiel 2:4.*

I was so frustrated by this strange repeated message and could not go back to sleep. Finally, I got up and went into the kitchen and made myself some tea. The Bible was still kind of mysterious to me at the time and although I read it on occasion, I had no clue about what this Ezekiel message might be.

I had not yet attended Seminary, and I did not know the Bible too well. In fact, I did not even know there was a book in the Bible called Ezekiel. But it did sound kind of Bible-like, so I picked up my Bible and turned to the index. Yep, there was an Ezekiel. Sipping my tea, I turned to that passage and read,

The people to whom I am sending you are obstinate and stubborn. Say to them, "This is what the Sovereign Lord says." But whether they listen to you or not—for they are a rebellious house—they will know that a prophet has been among them. (Ezekiel 2:4-5)

Crawling back into bed, I fell asleep thinking, *Well, that's strange? Those people are my friends. This couldn't have anything to do with tomorrow could it?* At the Bible study the next day, I showed up and shared my humble story of Africa with my state department friends. As I was sharing the Maasai healing story, a man stood up and literally shouted,

"Healing like this can't happen today! Those kind of miracles stopped when the apostles died." Another joined in to support his argument. I was shocked. I was hurt. Turns out these folks had been preparing a dispensational argument (a theological stance that God does not heal miraculously today as He did in the Bible) for weeks now. Of course, I did not know this. But Jesus did.

It was so very kind of Him to whisper this to me ahead of time, so when it happened, I would know He was with me. It is kind of a funny thing, but turns out these people from the state department got involved in ministry that involved healing and hearing God's voice a few short months after that night. God has a sense of humor, I am sure of it.

Not long after that, God called me away from Washington, D.C. to attend Fuller Seminary in Pasadena, California. Two months after I arrived, I met Ben, and we eventually married.

Ben and I moved to the Bay Area and both became pastors in the Presbyterian Church (USA). Eventually God led us to a big Presbyterian church in Menlo Park, California. One Sunday at Menlo Park Presbyterian, our preaching pastor, a former Stanford professor, was in the worship service with me. I shared with the congregation what I saw in Africa. I encouraged people that God is still in the business of healing people and speaking to ordinary people in amazing ways. Afterward Scott said to me,

"Christy, if I saw God heal like that or heard God speak in that way, I think my whole prayer life might change." Later, Scott was preaching while I was on maternity leave about the power of God to do things we do not always understand intellectually. After re-telling my experience in Africa, Scott said, "Now, I don't think Christy is a freak. Maybe she is though? Her husband Ben would know, I guess." The congregation roared with laughter because they knew I was just a normal, ordinary person, one of their pastors.

Well, I am really not a freak (though my kids and folks at the Wetlands might debate that some days). Jesus has graciously given me the gift of hearing His whispers. With His help, I have grown over time in discerning when the whispers I hear are God's voice and when they are just a spicy piece of pizza I ate last night.

Over time, I have learned to distinguish between what is the voice of the Lord, what is my own voice, and what is the voice of the enemy. My greatest joy is passing onto others what God has taught me about how to hear Him. I help people discern which whispers are God's whispers and which are coming from other sources.

We have a very real Enemy who lies to us all the time and beats us down. We need wisdom to know when that liar, Satan, is speaking to us, so we can bring into the light those messages that tear us down. Through God's power, we can silence them and finally be free to live the abundant life Jesus promises us (more on this in Chapter five).

We must walk humbly with our God and learn how to hear His voice if we want to walk in more power and live a strategic life for Jesus. Our time on this earth is very short and there are too many directions we can wander off in. There are too many people pulling us in the wrong direction and too many things that can distract and weigh us down. Jesus is speaking and wants to get through to us more loudly if we will let Him.

There are few things more important that hearing God speak to you in a personal way. Think about it. When you hear God whisper in a way that you know it is really the Living God speaking to you, all of life looks different. Suddenly, you have hope. You have fresh revelation. You will have the faith to face whatever hard things are confronting you in life. God delights in blowing apart the boxes we put around Him. The Lord longs to communicate with us in such a way that we can exclaim with wonder, "Jesus is here and He is real! I never knew He loved me this much and that He would talk with me in this special way."

Calling all ordinary people

One night after I put my kids to bed, I was up channel surfing before going to bed. I saw this funny show called, "Psychic Detectives." I rolled my eyes and thought, *Oh man, I gotta see what this show is all about!* It was about how psychics help the police figure out crimes. Yep, you read that right. This is really happening. Some of the most popular television shows these days are the psychic hot lines! Daily, millions of people tune into these shows and spend lots of money consulting psychics. Ever wonder why?

Human beings have a deep desire to believe they are not alone in the universe. They want to know there is someone out there with answers to the problems they are facing. They want to know there is someone who cares about their daily struggles and will actually speak direction into their lives. As Christ-followers, we know that there is someone whose name is Jesus, who by the power of the Holy Spirit, is more than able to speak words of love, direction, and guidance into our lives. The problem is the gap between what we know intellectually and what we actually experience in our normal, everyday lives.

So, let me ask you a question right now. If God began speaking to you in louder ways, what would it sound like? Would it be a big, booming voice?

Would it be a quiet whisper? Or perhaps a tougher question: If God wants to whisper to you more directly, are you open to hearing Him?

Each person who reads this book will be in a different place spiritually. Some of you are exploring the things of God and the concept of hearing the God of the Universe. You may think a whisper to you seems impossible. Others of you may have walked with God a long time but might feel distant from Him right now, overwhelmed with things in life, or just plain worn out.

I want to encourage you that it does not matter. Wherever you are on your spiritual journey, no matter how long you have known Jesus, no matter how far away you might feel from God, God wants to talk to you! God wants to deepen your prayer life so that you begin to experience more of His love. He wants you to hear His voice more personally and clearly. The Lord of the Universe wants to whisper to you. You are that important to Him.

I am going to invite you to do something. Can you think of a specific time when you can remember God speaking to you in some way? Maybe it was while reading a passage of Scripture and it was as if a verse jumped out at you and you knew God was speaking. Maybe it was watching a beautiful sunset and you felt God's peace wash over you. Perhaps it was in a tough time where the comfort of God came through a friend calling at just the exact moment you needed some encouragement. Maybe it was in a dream. Take a moment right now. Close your eyes and reflect on that time.

I am guessing that many of you remembered just such a moment. If you did remember a moment, I want to encourage you that you do hear God! Possibly, though, you wrote it off to a "nice feeling" or maybe just forgot about it. If that is you, please take a minute, and thank God for speaking to you in that moment. Be encouraged that the Lord, who has spoken to you in the past, has new things to whisper to you and that you can learn to discern His voice more than you have experienced so far in your life.

For those of you who could not remember a single moment or time when you think God may have spoken to you, please do not be discouraged. God is way better at getting through to you than you could ever be at hearing Him.

Whoever you are, whatever your name is, I can say this with confidence: God has things to say to you that will breathe new life into you. He knows the very things that are worrying you right now, and He cares about them, no matter how big or little they may seem. Without question, this loving God wants to teach you to hear His voice in new and deeper ways. *How do I know this?* you ask. It is the heart of God. He loves you more than you can imagine, and He longs to communicate with you. Walt Gerber, a former senior pastor at Menlo Park Presbyterian Church and mentor of mine, once commented,

"Our problem isn't that we believe God for too much, rather that we believe Him for too little." That is especially true when it comes to believing that God will whisper to us personally.

I have this amazing group of friends who pray for me constantly. They have committed to praying for each of you who are reading this book. We believe that as you read this book, God is going to surprise you and speak to you in ways that encourage you and lift you up. We are asking God to help you hear His voice. Maybe you have an area of your life that you need God's guidance? Perhaps you have always believed in God, but your faith has been more of an intellectual journey.

Consider that picking up this book is not just random but that it is God reaching out to you to help you hear His voice more clearly. Maybe you are weary, burned out, and you need a word of encouragement from Jesus that breathes faith where you feel hopeless. Maybe you feel so dry in your relationship with the Lord that you need Him to show up in a way that you say, like the blind man, "I was blind but now I see!" (John 9:25).

Our God is a big God. You can be sure that God knows exactly how to get through to you, in a voice that you can hear clearly. That part is for sure. Trusting God to speak to us. That is the hard part. Thankfully, God knows all about how hard it is for you to trust Him. And He is waiting for you to give him a window to show up and prove He is speaking to you.

GOD, PLEASE WHISPER TO ME NOW...

Right now, pause a moment. Pray and ask God to speak to you more directly, in a way that gets through to your heart.

What specific area of your life would you most like to hear God whisper to you about? Write it down below.

PRAYER

God, I need to hear your whispering voice. In this specific area of my life, I really need to hear you speak loudly to me over the noise.

(Take a moment of silence and give this area to God in your own words).

Lord, I'm asking you to turn up the volume so I can hear you on this need. Maybe you have something else to say to me? Help me to be open to hearing whatever you are saying to me. I confess that it is hard to bring this specific need to you. Some days it is hard to believe you are actually going to communicate with me about it. Increase my faith to believe you love me enough to speak about things that are important to me. Show me the way. Help me to hear your whispers. In Jesus' name. Amen.

.

3

Earplugs

We live in a world that has, for centuries now, cultivated the idea that the skeptical person is always smarter than the one who believes. You can be as dumb as cabbage as long as you doubt.
Dallas Willard, *Hearing God*

And without faith it is impossible to please God, because anyone who comes to him must believe that He exists and that He rewards those who earnestly seek Him.
Hebrews 11:6

Most of the time, my kids are pretty good friends. Other times, there can be some pretty heated arguments. When Benji was just six years old, I overheard a conflict going on between him and Annie, who was in the third grade at the time. My good friend, Cindy, says Annie could run a small country because she can be very persuasive with her words, and she is only 10 years old! That is a wonderful quality, but Benji would beg to differ when they are fighting.

On this particular Saturday morning, Annie was trying to convince Benji that he had done something wrong. Benji responded by covering his ears and shouting,

"Annie! I'm sick of your big third grade words! See? I can't even hear you. La La La!" It was pretty funny. Later, I thought to myself, Benji covering his ears was a perfect picture of what happens to us when we try to hear God.

Some of us have plugged ears when it comes to hearing God.

Most of the time, we do not cover our ears intentionally, but those earplugs are there even though we cannot see them. We may long for a deeper, more intimate relationship with Jesus where we can hear His voice more clearly, but our ears may be blocked and need to be unplugged so we can actually hear Him when He speaks! What are the names of those earplugs and just how can we remove them so we can hear God better? Good question.

Earplugs: 10 common blocks to hearing God's voice

In my travels speaking on hearing God's voice, I hear some pretty common hindrances. We all have them. These are the things that turn the volume down, so to speak, when it comes to hearing that quiet, gentle voice of the Living God. They are the "earplugs" that block the voice of God in our lives.

Listed below are my 10 biggies. As you read through them, I would invite you to consider which earplugs might be blocking you from hearing God's voice. You might even think of another earplug, and if you do, I would love to hear what earplug you discovered! Chances are, someone else is struggling with that very same blockage. Who knows, it might just help someone to know they are not alone in facing that particular hindrance. If you think of another that I did not mention, I would love to know, and you can send it to me at: www.christypierce.org.

1 · "That kind of stuff doesn't happen for me"

This is one of the biggies for sure. I cannot tell you how many times people approach me and say,

"Christy, I believe God probably speaks to people like Billy Graham or to my pastor. I just have trouble imagining He'd speak that clearly to me." When we operate with that assumption, we settle for less. One woman said it this way,

"I'm at this conference about hearing God whisper, and everyone else is having these great God moments. They hear God's voice, or see pictures, or get words, and I'm experiencing nothing!" She lamented in frustration, "It seems like God is speaking to everyone else but me."

When that happens, it can feel so discouraging that we often want to give up. We can feel "less than" others and even rejected by God. If that is you,

God has great compassion for you, and He does not want you to give up. He wants you to experience greater intimacy with Him and hear His voice more in your life. Do not believe this lie from the Enemy that "this kind of stuff doesn't happen" to you. God does speak to you, and He has led you to this book so that you will hear His voice in new ways. Do not give up. God has more of His abundant life that you have longed to experience.

2 · The head vs heart culture

Today we live in an intellectual, technological, and modern culture. There are good things about this, but bad things as well. When it comes to hearing God's voice, our culture itself can be a huge earplug! We live in the Western, scientific world of a you-have-to-see-it-to-believe-it mentality. The spiritual world of the unseen is difficult for us to comprehend.

Typically, as Westerners, we are an intellectual bunch, less comfortable with things of the Spirit. One Sunday night at New Hope Peninsula Church, our prayer team was in the sanctuary praying before the service. Unexpectedly, the computer system crashed, and all the sound, video, and computer equipment went down.

Fortunately, we live in Silicon Valley and have high-tech folks in our congregation who practically invented computers. They went to work on the system. No dice. Nothing they tried worked. These were the best of the best when it comes to technical stuff. But nothing was working. A humble, quiet woman in our prayer team was watching. She approached the team and said,

"I think the problem may have something to do with these wires." They dismissed her (politely, of course), essentially giving her the "thanks, but no thanks" response. They kept working on the mess of cords before them. The woman quietly walked over to the wires she mentioned, picked them up, and prayed. Bingo! All systems started up and kept going. Our technical team loves this story. They said it taught them a lot about hearing God's voice, and of course, about humility.

Here is another question I get from people when I speak about the whispers of God. It goes something like this,

"Christy, I've been a Christian all my life, and if God really speaks to people like this, what's wrong with my relationship that I'm not hearing His voice this way?" Good question, but I might suggest it is the wrong one to ask. It is not that there is something wrong with your relationship with God, but instead, that Jesus wants more for you.

Consequently, a better question to ask is, "Lord, will you speak to me more?" My guess is you have actually heard the whispering voice of God, you just did not realize this was really Jesus speaking personally to you. There is always more God has for you if you want to hear Him. The Bible challenges all of us not to be satisfied with where we are in our faith, but to press on and to take hold of all that Christ Jesus has for us (Philippians 3:14).

Taking the hand of Jesus, in humility, should require all of us to want all He wants for us, to want more of Him. The best use of our energies is not to defend why we may not have heard Him more clearly in our lives until now. Instead, God gently urges us to be open to new experiences with Him. God is a gentleman. If we do not want more of Him, He will not barge into our lives. If we draw near to God, asking Him to speak to us more, that is a prayer God delights in answering.

3 · Fear of hearing wrong

We live in a culture obsessed with perfectionism. We preach about grace, but we can get caught up in the "fear of being wrong." We can get paralyzed by fear of making a mistake and cease to believe God could actually speak new things to us. How can we know we are really hearing from God? Could it just be an active imagination? What if we get it wrong? We are so bound up by our need to be perfect that we struggle with giving ourselves permission to open ourselves to new experiences of hearing God's voice.

Plus, there is a whole other fear of being labeled as weird! We do not want to be labeled as a freak where nonsense spills out and offends a good friend, right? We do believe God speaks, but we do not want to make mistakes on God's behalf. And we certainly do not want to make a mistake that ends up making us look like a freak.

If you struggle with the perfectionism earplug, I have some good news and some bad news for you. Here is the bad news: You will get it wrong. The Bible is clear that we are not on the same level as the Old Testament prophets, who had direct downloads from God. You might hear a word and find it really was the bad piece of pizza, or the Enemy, or just your own voice.

And yet, that is actually part of the good news. You will hear incorrectly sometimes, but that is how you will learn to discern His voice. I want to challenge you not to let that stop you. Please do not shrink back from the "more" God wants for you when it comes to hearing His voice. I love that the Apostle Paul, in perhaps the messiest church ever when it comes to hearing God wrong, still urged the people not to give up on hearing God's voice. He wrote, "Follow the way of love, and eagerly desire spiritual gifts, especially the gift of prophecy" (1 Corinthians 14:1).

Paul's words encourage us that even though we will not hear God with 100 percent accuracy, we should still press into having an intimate relationship with the Living God, where we learn to hear Him. He wrote, "Now we see but a poor reflection in a mirror; but then we shall see face to face" (1 Corinthians 13:12). Yes, we will make mistakes, but as John exhorted us: "Test the spirits to see whether they are from God" (1 John 4:1).

John seemed to know there would be interference. But, if we walk in humility as we seek to hear God, we will learn through our mistakes. Think about it. What would happen if every new preacher who gave a bad sermon was told that their sermon stunk and they should give up? What would happen if those trying to serve the homeless made a bad sandwich or said the wrong thing? No one says, "Stop it! Make better peanut butter and jelly next time, and be sure you know the exact quote of Scripture before you try!"

You cannot let your fear of getting it wrong block you from hearing God. Of course, there are some very good safeguards about how pastors and leaders can protect their churches from well-meaning Christians who get imbalanced in hearing God. We will get to that in chapters nine and 10. But there is no way I can point you to experiencing hearing God's voice in some new, life-changing ways without being willing to step out in faith and risk making a mistake or two along the way. The good news is that God is bigger than our mistakes. It is totally possible to hear God, and then to share what we hear in a way that is balanced, biblical, humble, and filled with grace.

4 · Fear

Face it: Some of us are just plain afraid of hearing God. Frequently, I hear people confess their secret fears as they lament,

"Christy, what if God tells me to sell everything I own and go to Africa?" Or, another worry that scares people:

"What if God reads my mail in front of everybody, and He starts yelling at me about my mistakes? I'm afraid I don't want to hear God!" Many people who suffer from this earplug are worried that when God speaks to them, it will be a condemning, judgmental message. I love to burst that fear bubble!

If you struggle with fear, I want to encourage you that God loves you more than you could imagine in your wildest dreams. If you open yourself to hearing Him more, you can count on His heart opening toward you. Time and time again, I watch people who are taking courageous steps of faith to reach out with these worried looks on their faces, braced for a harsh word from God. They are often blown away when they hear God speak the just the opposite! God always shows up tenderly, with great compassion, and speaks a loving word that sets them free from fear. As 1 John 4:18 says,

"Perfect love drives out fear." Nothing defeats the earplug of fear like God's love. The fear that God will shame is a lie from the Enemy. While it is true that God cares about areas of sin in our lives, He is much more concerned that we understand how much we are loved. Isaiah declares,

"God's kindness leads you to repentance" (Romans 2:4). It is also very common for people to be afraid of asking God to speak to them for fear they will be disappointed by silence. Dear friends, that is another huge lie of the Enemy. I have seen people reach out to God for the first time, desperately hoping He will talk to them, and God breaks into their life with a loving picture, word, or image that brings them joy. He does not fail.

5 · Pain

My family has been through two very pain-filled, traumatic years in emergency rooms and hospital stays. Those years are the headlines of our suffering, but I will tell you the detailed version later. For now, let me point out what you already know: No one will escape suffering in this life. Painful relationships, traumatic events, and the devastating effects of living in this broken world with sinful people will all hit us in some way. When it does, it can literally knock the wind out of us and devastate our lives.

You may be in that kind of pain right now. If you are, you need to know that God weeps when you weep. What I do know about pain is this: God does not waste pain. The good news about our suffering is that God will always use it for our ultimate good if we press into Him and ask for good to come about.

It is a strange paradox, but few things can teach us to hear God's whisper more than pain. Pain can either block us from hearing God or be the very thing that opens our ears to God's whispers more than we have ever experienced in our lives. Yes, despite crippling pain and suffering, there is good news in the midst of it. No matter what you feel, God is there for you, and He is able to reach you in your pain. He is better at reaching you in your pain than you are at reaching out for Him. Scripture says, "He is close to the brokenhearted and saves those who are crushed in spirit" (Psalm 34:18). It is often right at our point of pain when we cry out to God and hear Him whisper. If pain is an earplug for you, I want to encourage you to press into God. Know that He is there to comfort you and to meet you in your pain. Do not be afraid to let Him in.

6 · Sin

Recently, I was doing a Whispers of God conference in Oregon. I asked the attendees to help me think of barriers to hearing God's voice in their own life. One brave woman said it simply,

"Sin." I reflected on this and realized she was right. We can do our own ear-plugging from hearing God's voice if we are continuing in patterns of sin that are preventing us from the intimate relationship God wants for us. When my son, Benji, was two years old, he threw some really impressive tantrums. When he was angry, he was pretty cute with that blond hair and freckled face turning so red. He was also very loud. Since he could not express his feelings in words yet, he would use his body, namely his little fists, to try to hit his sisters, yelling loudly,

"No! No! No!" Truthfully, my family did not think it was so cute when it happened. We would take him to a quiet place of timeout until he calmed down. We loved him in these moments, however, no less than in the moments when he was happy and calm. God is like that. If we are persisting in sin, he loves us no less, but He may put us in timeout for a spell.

The good news is this: If God only wanted to speak to perfect people, there would be no one for Him to communicate with in human history. The Bible is clear: "For all have sinned and fall short of the glory of God" (Romans 3:23). Instead, this earplug of sin I am referring to is regarding those persistent sin patterns that we are trapped in and cannot seem to stop.

These things can limit our ability to hear God. We cannot get on with the business of deep communion and intimacy with Him because our sin is in the way. A friend of mine is a deeply devout Christian who has an alcohol addiction. One day, she came to me in tears. She said,

"Christy, I've tried and tried to give up drinking, but I keep failing, then spiraling into self-hatred. The worst part is, every time I fail, I feel like God hates me." She confessed, "I know that's not true in my head, but in my heart, I somehow feel 'blocked' from hearing God when I'm in that pattern." We spent months praying, and she joined Alcoholics Anonymous (AA). After a few months of AA and people praying for her weekly, the Lord delivered her from this alcoholic lifestyle. For the first time since I had known her, her eyes were filled with joy and she had hope. Not only that, she was regularly experiencing God speaking to her in some extraordinary ways as she prayed.

God wants us to be free. When we choose to continue in patterns of sin, we will limit our ability to hear Him. When we continue to hold onto anger, resentment or unforgiveness, it is like driving a car with dirty windows. It is hard to see clearly. But, through repentance we can clean those windows. In the Hebrew, repentance literally means to "turn back." When we turn back to God, and ask for forgiveness, He always freely gives it. Then our intimacy with Him is restored, and the lines of communication are opened more fully to God's voice and leading.

7 · Pride

If I had to pick which earplug blocks our ears the most, it would be this one: pride. Pride is so subtle, and it likes to hide. Often people will ask me, "Why is it that God moves so powerfully in India or Africa, but we don't hear God speak as much here in our country?" I will not pretend to have all the answers, but I can respond by sharing my own personal struggle with the pride earplug. Despite being a speaker on God's whispers, I can get blocked thinking I can do things on my own, and before I know it, drift away from God.

Subconsciously, I can get trapped into thinking I do not need God that much. I sometimes get so busy doing the work of God, I forget to get on my knees and remember the truth He spoke, "Apart from Me, you can do nothing" (John 15:5).

The pride earplug can also disguise itself in different forms. I regularly encounter people at my Whispers of God conferences with skeptical faces, crossed arms, and closed hearts. I can tell that their issues are not about honest questions and doubt. One of my favorite Bible heroes is Thomas, who was brave enough to be real in his doubt and ask God for proof that Jesus was resurrected. Some might feel he had little faith, but it makes me feel better to know that even one of Jesus' disciples had doubts.

Pride, however, is not about doubt, common to all men. Pride is about a belief in the absolute "right" way, or perfect theology, when it comes to experiencing God. People who struggle with this earplug are not interested in new ways of knowing God and often will say privately to me,

"This whisper stuff might be great for other people, Christy, but I'm satisfied with going to church Sunday, reading my Bible and listening to my preacher hear God for the people. That's good enough for me." When I hear these kind of things, it literally makes my heart hurt.

I believe that is because God is allowing me to feel the way it feels to Him. God wants to talk to His children, if we will only have learner's hearts. Of course, hearing God through the Bible and through good preaching is fantastic. The Bible is one of the primary ways God will speak to us. Going to church and hearing God's Word preached is another key way. For 20 years, I have been preaching the Word, teaching the Bible, and leading worship. Let me assure you, I affirm good preaching, Bible study, and hearing God's word in church worship services. At the same time, when I see a spirit of pride, which prevents people from experiencing more of God's presence and power in their lives, it breaks my heart. The sad truth is that if we choose to limit the ways God can speak to us, He will not bust through those barricades in our hearts. It is hard to hear God whisper when we think we have all we need. People with open hearts and ears are those who open the door to God's presence and voice guiding their lives.

8 · Our technology-driven, fast-paced culture

When it comes to hearing God, does technology help or hurt us? E-mails, iPhones, texts, Facebook, Instagram, Twitter, and other high-tech ways of communicating are great at keeping us connected to people, but they get in the way of us hearing the quiet whispers of God.

Every day, we zoom around multi-tasking by moving from our e-mails to texts to phone calls to Siri navigating us to the next meeting. Hearing God in the chaos becomes practically impossible. Honestly, some days I want to toss my cellphone into the Bay on purpose!

Not long ago, I was sitting in Starbucks working on a sermon and talking to my husband, Ben, on my cellphone. We were going through the day's schedule. Who was going to do the carpool? Who was going to speak at the prayer meeting? What time was dinner? Who is preaching this week, and who is going to the soccer game? It was just the usual, crazy schedule. All of a sudden, I felt a hand on my shoulder. I turned around and was shocked to see it was Ben. He said to me with a smile on his face,

"What's wrong with this picture?" We were too busy to notice we were sitting right next to one another. As a mom of three young children, a pastor, a writer, and a speaker, some days I barely have time to go to the bathroom, much less pray! I have found that if I want to hear God whisper, I have to make time.

Frequently, I have to get up at five a.m. just to be with Jesus and get into His presence. This helps me survive my busy days and love the people around me. If I want an ongoing conversational relationship with the Living God, I truly must make time to simply be with Him. Sabbath has become as important as eating and drinking to me.

If Jesus had to withdraw to quiet and lonely places to pray and hear His Father, how much more do we need to stop the chaos and find quiet places to seek Him? The good news is that God knows we are fragile and weak. If we give God even a small window, He rushes in to meet with us. God is very kind that way, and He longs to hang out with us. That is how much He wants to communicate with you.

9 · The Enemy

You have a very real Enemy who does not want you to hear God's challenging and encouraging voice. In fact, this may be the greatest external block you have when it comes to hearing God. This liar, Satan, does not want you to hear God. Instead, he is constantly trying to block your ears from hearing the loving voice of God. The Bible is very clear that Satan is on a mission to "kill, steal, and destroy" (John 10:10); he is the "father of lies" (John 8:44). In fact, the Enemy may be lying to you right this very minute.

Satan may be speaking lies even now like, *You can't hear God. This 'God whispering' stuff isn't for real. Don't start thinking you'll actually hear the voice of God for yourself because you know the secret sin in your life. What makes you think God would actually talk to you?* If you are hearing this kind of garbage, do me a favor: Tell him to shut up. I mean it. Do it right now. Even if you are not sure if it is the Enemy or yourself, even if you are not sure what you think about Satan, please just humor me. Tell those voices to be silent and see what happens.

My friend, Mike, says that all of us have at least one lie we believe about ourselves. I agree, and most of us probably have more than one lie that we beat ourselves up with daily. What are the lies that you believe about yourself? The Enemy's mission is to discourage you, to lie to you, and to tear you down. The last thing the Enemy wants is for you to learn how to hear God's whispers of love to you.

Think about it. If you learn to hear God speak to you about the things that matter in your life, you will overcome the Enemy, and he will become less relevant in your life. Even when you are anxious, you can hear the voice of God and have peace. When you are afraid, you can experience His very-near presence and hear a word or see a picture, and you experience God freeing you from that fear that held you captive. Instead of falling into a pit of despair and discouragement, you can hear God whisper, *I love you. I'm for you. Cry out to me, and I will help you.* Now, I ask you, do you think the Enemy wants you to hear these encouraging and loving messages from God? No way! When you begin to hear God whisper to you, and you fall more in love with Jesus as He does that, the Enemy is furious. His plans to mess with you and to discourage you are defeated. God's voice becomes louder, and the dark voices are drowned out by the booming voice of your Father in heaven who loves you passionately. (As a side note: We will talk practical strategies for defeating the Enemy's whispers in chapter 10.)

10 · "We don't know how"

Many people would really like to hear God more in their lives and are even willing to learn new ways of hearing God, but they simply do not know where to start. If that is your earplug, I have good news for you. I am going to give you specific steps on how you can be yourself and still hear God. In the chapters ahead, my hope is that you will discover you do not need a Ph.D. to hear God, just a willing heart! God knows just how to get through to you, and with a few new tools and a God-breathed faith, you will see it is possible to hear God more clearly.

GOD, PLEASE WHISPER TO ME NOW...

Consider the 10 barriers mentioned in this chapter that tone down hearing God's voice in our lives. We all have at least one earplug. As you reflect, which earplugs might be affecting your hearing God more? Take a minute and circle those that might be impacting you. Can you think of others not on the list? Write that down too!

Ten earplugs that hinder God's voice
1 · "That kind of stuff doesn't happen for me"
2 · Head vs. heart culture
3 · Fear of hearing wrong
4 · Fear
5 · Pain
6 · Sin
7 · Pride
8 · Our technology-driven and fast-paced culture
9 · The Enemy
10 · "We don't know how"

PRAYER

Lord, I do want to hear your voice more clearly. Please help break down this barrier starting today, so that I will have greater ability to hear You. Thank you that no earplug is too big for you to remove. Please, God, remove all blocks because I do want to hear you speak to me. In the name of Jesus I pray, Amen.

Who Is Whispering?

And after the fire came a gentle whisper.
1 Kings 19:12

The wonderful news is that Jesus has not stopped acting and speaking. He is resurrected and at work in our world. He is not idle, nor has he developed laryngitis.
Richard Foster, *Celebration of Discipline*

My husband loves to travel. He is what you would call an airplane junkie. As a former missionary in Africa, he loves to travel anywhere, anytime. In fact, the longer the plane trip, the better. We spent the first years of our marriage flying around the world doing mission trips. A problem arose when we had kids, and unlike someone without a travel-addiction, Ben refused to buy in to the idea that they could not go with us. (Those of you who have flown with your own children or next to kids on planes get it!)

Several years ago, Ben talked me into taking our two-year-old, Corey, and our six-month-old, Annie, to Scotland for a family reunion. Annie decided to stay awake all the way to Europe. In fact, she did not sleep at all for 36 hours. Once in Scotland, Annie decided to sleep during the day and stay up at night. Now, I am sure Scotland is a lovely place, but it was a blur to me. On our way home, I was so wiped out we decided to stop in New York City to check into a hotel and sleep. We managed to get our luggage, two sleep-deprived babies, and ourselves onto the hotel shuttle.

When we arrived at the hotel, I staggered off the bus with one mission: get to a quiet, dark room and sleep. As I entered the hotel, I heard God whisper quietly, *Christy, tell the bus driver this: The Lord says you have the faith of Elijah and will change the hearts of many.*

Now, you have to understand when I say, "I heard God whisper," I mean it sounds like a whisper, a very quiet voice in my head. Over time, I have learned how to tune in to those quiet whispers and sense what is really God and what is not. (We will unpack this in detail in chapter nine.) On this particular morning at a New York City airport hotel, this was a very faint, quiet whisper. So quiet, in fact, that I was about to ignore it, block it out, and march to my hotel room to sleep.

I began to complain to God with a truly faith-filled response: *God, this isn't really you right? You know how tired I am. I'm probably hearing things because I'm sleep deprived and delirious!* Convinced I must be wrong about this whisper, I turned and started to walk into the hotel. But I heard God whisper again: *Christy, tell that man that he has the faith of Elijah and will change the hearts of many.* I glanced at this African-American man, hunched over carrying bags, and I could not leave. So, I slowly walked over, saying to myself, *OK God, I hope this is you.* I tapped him on the shoulder and as he turned to me, just waiting, I took a deep breath and said,

"Hi there. This may seem really weird, but as I was leaving I think God may have said something to me about you. It may seem strange, so if it doesn't mean anything to you, no worries." I paused again, taking yet another deep breath, "But here is what I think I heard God whisper to me to tell you: The Lord says you have the faith of Elijah and will change the hearts of many."

This sweet man stopped loading the bags and tears filled his eyes. He told me to wait a minute, and he ran onto the shuttle bus. He came back with a tattered Bible and said,

"Ma'am I can't believe this. I've followed Jesus all my life. But these past years, well, I fell away. I have been on drugs and left my family. Just yesterday I came back to Him, told Him I wanted to come clean." He hung his head as he continued, "I told God I wanted him to take control of my life and please take me back. I just didn't know if God would take me back after all I have done wrong."

Early that morning in New York City, God whispered to a weary bus driver who needed a touch of His love. At the same time, God breathed life back into a tired, weary mother who needed to know that God was indeed real and loved her.

So, how did I know it was God? How did I know that God was speaking those words about a stranger's Elijah-like faith and that it was not merely the product of the multiple-day sleep debt I was working up? How do we know when it is God speaking and when, well, it just is not?

Do you know <u>who</u> is whispering to you?

Several years ago, I was invited to speak at a women's conference in Bel Air, California. It was a lovely ocean setting, and God was moving powerfully. One night, the prayer ministers on my team spent three hours praying with women—until they were finally kicked out of the bar where they were praying at midnight! These women had real, interactive encounters with the God who whispers and heard God speak to them in ways they never imagined. Women were coming to faith in Jesus as they experienced God whisper truths through the prayer warriors that only God could know. The morning after this wonderful night, we were gathered together in a large hotel room. I was taking questions from the women and attempting to answer their excellent questions about how we know it is really God speaking. One woman stood up in the back and said very humbly,

"Christy, I need your help to discern God's voice. You see, before I became a Christ-follower, I was a psychic. How do I know what is God's voice, what is my voice, and what is the Enemy's voice?" Talk about a great question! I was so glad she was bold enough to ask that in front of all those churched women.

It took guts, and her question spoke to the fears many people (especially Christians) have when it comes to hearing God. In Chapter nine, I will get very specific about how you can discern what is God's voice, what is your own voice, and what is from the Enemy. We will talk about safeguards when it comes to hearing God's voice and how to do this stuff in grounded, biblical ways that will hopefully help Christians stay balanced and humble.

That is important. What I want to emphasize in this chapter is that we need to know who is speaking to us.

My view is that the God who is whispering to you is the same God of the Bible. I have had people push back on me about this and say things like, "Well, I hear God speak all the time, and I don't know if I believe in Jesus." There is certainly biblical precedent for God speaking to people who are not yet followers of Jesus. Saul on the Damascus road comes immediately to mind. And as I listen to my missionary friends they tell me that many of the Muslims who are coming to Christ around the world have experienced God appearing to them in dreams, visions, and in the miraculous. Many can come to Christ no other way.

What I do know is that no matter what God is speaking by His Holy Spirit, He does not say things that contradict what He has already spoken in His written Word. God is not forgetful. He is the same yesterday, today, and forever, and even when speaking to 21st century Christians who are facing situations never imagined in the pages of Scripture, what He says today will be consistent with the things He has always said. More in chapter nine, but I wanted to lay down a few principles here. My response is that I believe it is the Spirit of the Living God, of Jesus, through the Holy Spirit that Jesus promised would speak to us when He left this earth.

Whether or not someone believes in Jesus does not change how much He loves him or her, and He is constantly pursuing with a whispering voice of love. Jesus is a Living God who still speaks to those who will listen. What I typically say to people with these types of questions is something like this, "God loves you, and I would invite you to ask God to reveal Himself to you. The Spirit of God speaks to people differently, but He made you." I tell them, "Before you were formed in your mother's womb, He created you, and He knows you like no one else does. Ask God to show you who He is."

In an age where people claim to have all sorts of spiritual experiences hearing "voices," Christians need to understand the biblical foundation for hearing God's voice speaking to them. Lots of voices are constantly trying to get our attention, and it is important to learn how to discern what is the real voice of God, and what is the spicy piece of pizza we ate last night! (Chapter nine will discuss this in detail.) For now, let me emphasize that we need to know the Bible. We need to be people who are devoted to understanding the written Word of God and applying it to our daily lives.

Wherever you are in your spiritual journey, I think it is important to be honest and upfront about my views of the God who is whispering. If we are seeking the God who whispers, we should know whom we are seeking. By now, I hope you can sense that I am a person who values being honest, transparent and real. Remember, I told you I am done with my Washingtonian-politically-correctness! So, I am going to be really direct about just who I believe is the One speaking to you with that gentle voice. You might not fully agree with me, and that is OK. But I would invite you to think about these things, because we are not seeking a "spiritual experience" or just trying to hear any random voice. Instead, we are seeking a very real God who does, in fact, speak to His people. This God is love. This God is a God who is constantly seeking after the children that He created, and is always trying to communicate with them in a way that makes sense to them. But just who is that God? That is the question we must all wrestle with at some point in our lives.

The God who whispers is a Living God. To truly understand who the Spirit of God is who whispers to people today, we must go back to the book that God, Himself, wrote: The Bible.

It is really critical that we understand God whispering from the foundation of the Bible. Therefore, this chapter is about understanding the God who whispers from the book He wrote, the Bible. We can learn so much from understanding God's written word that will guide us in our journey of hearing God whisper.

1 · The Bible teaches us that God speaks to ordinary people

I could take this entire book to tell the stories of how God spoke to ordinary people throughout human history. However, there is a way better book to read if we want to do that—uh, the Bible! I would encourage you to read it, and if you do, you will notice there is story after story of God speaking to ordinary people. God spoke to Adam and Eve in the garden in Genesis two. The Lord spoke to Noah and commanded him to build an ark in Genesis six. God spoke to Abraham and called him to leave his home and go to a land he did not yet know in Genesis 12. In Genesis 15, God told Abraham and

Sarah they would have children even though Sarah's womb was barren. Isaiah heard the voice of the Lord and cried out, "Woe to me! ... I am ruined! For I am a man of unclean lips, and I live among a people of unclean lips, and my eyes have seen the King, the Lord Almighty" (Isaiah 6:5). In the New Testament, Mary heard God speak that she would become pregnant with the Savior of the world and chose to believe God: "For nothing is impossible with God" (Luke 1:37).

The list goes on and on. We consider the people of the Bible to be heroes who had very personal encounters with God and heard His voice. And yet, Richard Foster notes in his book, *The Celebration of Discipline,*

"God spoke to them not because they had special abilities, but because they were willing to listen" (16). The Bible is full of God speaking to ordinary people from the days of Adam and Eve until the book of Revelation. God clearly speaks to ordinary men, women, and children. Why would God stop now? Christians proclaim that Jesus Christ "is the same yesterday, today and tomorrow," and Jesus is still speaking today as He was then.

2 · The Bible also reminds us that God constantly chooses imperfect people to whisper to in life

If you read your Bible, you will soon discover this wonderful repeated pattern: God speaks to ordinary people who are not perfect at all! One of my favorite stories of God whispering in the Bible is the real life story of Elijah found in 1 Kings 19. You may know the story. Right before this passage, Elijah has been what I would call "a Rambo for God."

Taking on 450 prophets of Baal by himself, God shows up in power through Elijah. God validates Elijah and this hero in the faith calls down fire on all the false prophets. Elijah shows us what it means to really believe God has whispered to you and then to bravely step out in faith, even if it means death. Now, here is the part of the story I love the best! (Maybe that is because I have a Ph.D. in anxiety and have days when I am more fearful than fearless!) After Elijah experienced the incredible power of God move through him to defeat all those prophets of Baal, a solitary woman, Jezebel, threatens to kill him.

I am not sure why, but Elijah becomes fearful. It may be kind of scary to get a death threat, but he just stood up to 450 prophets of Baal in front of huge crowds of people and laughed in their faces. Jezebel is only one woman, and Elijah has seen God deliver him from threatening mobs—first-hand! Whatever the reason for the fear, I am grateful for it. Elijah has a first-class meltdown, starts running for his life and rants and raves at God. He is burned out, weary, and has had enough. Elijah cries out to God,

"I have had enough, Lord," he said, "Take my life; I am no better than my ancestors" (1 Kings 19:4). After Elijah vents to the Lord, he falls asleep, exhausted. At this very moment, we see a very real man: scared, exhausted, and not sure God will come through for him.

Do you ever feel like that? I sure do. No matter how many times I have heard God speak, seen God heal, or do real-life miracles, I still get scared. I still get burned out and exhausted. It is so comforting to know that this hero of the faith was also an ordinary man, who had his own moments of meltdown. Enter the tenderness of God. The Lord does not look down on Elijah for his little faith. Instead, God sends an angel to take care of him in his exhaustion, bringing food, sleep, and a place of safety. At Mount Horeb, Elijah is restored to a place where he can heal, recover, and hear God speak again. This time, God speaks in the way that He usually speaks: in a quiet whisper. After the fire, God spoke to Elijah through the gentle whisper (1 Kings 19:12).

Here lies one of the most important lessons in the Bible when it comes to hearing God's voice. Most of the time, God does not speak in a loud, dramatic voice. Most of the time, God does not shout with a booming voice from heaven. Most of the time, God's voice is not like thunder or fire. Most of the time, it is a gentle whisper. God loves to whisper to His people. He especially loves whispering to those of us who are battered by life, who are weary carrying heavy loads, and who feel far away our Abba Father. Elijah was a man just like us. I am an ordinary, broken person, but God delights in using ordinary people to do His will. He loves to whisper to all of us who will listen. Someone once said that it takes more faith to believe that God does not exist than to believe that He exists. That same argument holds true when it comes to the biblical evidence that ordinary people can hear God's voice.

3 · Because of Jesus, all believers have a right to an intimate relationship with God where we can learn to hear His voice

In the Old Testament, the Holy Spirit had not yet been poured out on the people of God. The Lord tended to work by speaking in an intense and focused way to prophets, kings, judges, or other leaders who would hear Him for the people and lead them accordingly. That is not to say that others did not have deep and sincere faith. (Remember Mary and Joseph? They were neither priests nor judges, but yet God spoke directly to them.) However, the norm for most followers of Yahweh at that time was to live somewhat at a distance from Him and the things He might want to say to them.

When Moses' face shone from being in God's presence, the people had to turn away from him. God's people had to keep a distance from the holy mountain where Moses received the Ten Commandments. The Holy of Holies and the thick curtain that separated it from the rest of the temple illustrate how the "norm" in Israel was for a spiritual life heavily mediated through leaders.

All of that began to change when Jesus came. Even though Jesus was God, everything about how He interacted with people and spoke to His Father foreshadowed that God was turning the page on how He would relate to people from that time forward. Jesus was approachable; He loved the unlovely; He healed the broken and outcast. Many tax collectors, prostitutes, and sinners who found no place for themselves in the religious system previously began flocking to Jesus. He gave off a vibe of love and acceptance. He called God "Abba," "Daddy," and the New Testament tells us in Romans 8:15 that we can too!

Jesus related to people with the same welcome the father gave to the prodigal when he came home (Luke 15:22-24). It was with open arms, forgiveness, and without condemnation that Jesus invited people into relationship with him. The only people Jesus seemed to have trouble with were those who were too proud of themselves, their status, or their religious systems to come to God on the basis of grace. When Jesus died on the cross, He made the way possible for us to have an intimate relationship with a Holy God because He paid the price for our sins on the cross.

For all of us who believe in Him, His death and resurrection means that we have eternal life, and we can have a close, intimate relationship with the Father through His sacrifice. Because of Jesus, we have intimate access to the Father. In Romans 8:15-17 we are told,

> For you did not receive a spirit that makes you a slave again to fear, but you received a Spirit of adoption. And by him we cry, Abba Father. The Spirit testifies with our spirit that we are God's children. Now if we are children, then we are heirs—heirs of God and coheirs with Christ, if indeed we share in his sufferings in order that we may also share in his glory.

It is only because of Jesus that we can even talk about God whispering to people. Jesus gave all believers the ability to draw near to God and to hear Him personally in our lives, because He went to the cross to die for our sins. Because of His death on the cross, and resurrection from the dead, we are given the right to be children of God. We are given the incredible privilege of a personal relationship with a Holy God where we can talk with Him intimately. Paul writes, "Let us draw near to God with a sincere faith, in full assurance of faith..." (Hebrews 10:22).

Jesus said, "I have called you friends" (John 15:15). Friends talk to friends. It is not a detached relationship He is after with us. Even the great hymns we sing testify to God speaking to us, "He walks with me, and He talks with me, and He tells me I am His own" (Charles Austin Miles, *In the Garden,* 1912).

4 · The Bible teaches us that God will speak to us through the Holy Spirit.

The Day of Pentecost changed everything for Christ's followers. Jesus had said that His followers were not to leave Jerusalem at first because they did not yet have the power they needed to spread his love. That power would come once the Spirit was given to them.

Pentecost was the day when this amazing outpouring came to pass. Tongues of fire signifying the Holy Spirit came to rest on everyone who believed in Jesus. Intimacy with God was no longer something only leaders experienced and mediated to the people. From that day forward, the normal *modus operandi* of following God changed. "Normal" was now that anyone who believed in Jesus was also filled with His Holy Spirit.

In fact, Romans 8:9 says that without the Spirit living us, we cannot truly be followers of Christ. Let me say that again. The New Testament lays out the pattern that having the Holy Spirit within us is no longer solely in the domain of leaders and VIPs. It is the baseline, ground zero, where the Christian life starts for all of his people. God speaks to us through His written word, and also through the Holy Spirit. As Christians, we claim that Jesus is the Living God, who can be known personally. He is a God who still communicates with His children. In that way, Christianity is unique from all other religions. We believe in Jesus Christ, who was not just a prophet who walked on this earth 2000 years ago and is now just another dead guy. Not in the slightest. He is Lord. He rose from the dead and promised that for all who put his or her faith in Him, He would send to them a Helper, the Holy Spirit, who would come to us and be our Counselor here on this earth.

But I tell you the truth: It is for your good that I am going away. Unless I go, the Counselor will not come to you; but if I go, I will send him to you. But when he, the Spirit of truth, comes, he will guide you into all truth. (John 16:7, 13)

Yes, the Bible is clear that while the Scriptures are a tremendous gift and powerful tool when it comes to knowing about Jesus and hearing God, they also remind us that the written Word is not the only way in which God speaks to His people.

What do YOU think?

Can I ask you to stop a minute and ask yourself some questions that are really critical for your faith journey: Do you want to hear the gentle voice of God speaking to you? If God is whispering to you, do you want to learn how to tune into that quiet, gentle voice more in your life? I am convinced that there are few things in the Christian journey that are more important than learning to hear God's voice.

What could be more important than hearing the Lord speak to you in such a way that you just "knew that you knew" this is really God? There is a famous chapter of the Bible in the book of Hebrews. You may have read it, and you may have even heard countless sermons on it. We preachers often refer to it as, "the Faith chapter." Hebrews chapter 11 tells us,

"Now faith is being sure of what we hope for and certain of what we do not see" (Hebrews 11:1). The Bible then cites an exhaustive list of people who did heroic things for God. They were men and women who had great faith and believed God at His very word. I have preached from this text many times and have heard many great sermons on faith from it. The interesting thing is that few of these sermons point out something really critical when it comes to how God whispers: Hebrews 11 shows us that perhaps the greatest act of faith among these great names was their belief that the voice they were hearing was truly God. They had faith to believe that the God of the Universe would actually speak to them, and then they stepped out believing that whisper, despite often risking their lives to do so. Wow!

With all this evidence in Scripture, I would submit to you that it takes more faith to believe that God does not want to speak to you than to believe He does. If that is true, then why is it so hard for people today to believe God wants to speak to them personally? Richard Foster points out one of the reasons for this struggle when he writes,

> Human beings seem to have a perpetual tendency to have somebody else talk to God for them. We are content to have the message second-hand. The history of religion is the story of an almost desperate scramble to have a king, a mediator, a priest, a pastor, a go-between. In this way we do not need to go to God ourselves. Such an approach saves us from the need to change, for to be in the presence of God is to change. (Celebration of Discipline, page 24)

One time, I was speaking in Oregon, and after I finished talking about whispers of God, a very honest man pulled me aside and said,

"Christy, I believe God speaks. It's just that I believe He speaks to His people through Scripture, through the Bible, through good sermons or as we serve the poor." I agreed wholeheartedly! At the same time, if we say that is the only way God speaks, we are putting God in a box. By the way, this is a box that God did not live in even during the days of the writers of the Bible.

If we choose this paradigm of how God speaks, we are missing a few very real ways that the Lord relates to His people. God has so much more for those of you who want to hear God more personally in your day-to-day life. God is always challenging us to come closer, to go deeper, and to taste and see more of Him.

God will speak to you through the Bible

Reading your Bible and hearing God speak through Scripture are going to be some of the most important ways God speaks to you. Perhaps you have had experiences of doing a Bible study or reading your Bible, and it was as if God had taken a holy yellow highlighter and a certain verse seemed to jump off the page. During a quiet time, have you ever had a moment when, as you read a passage of Scripture, a gentle peace washed over you and you realized it was God speaking to you? God can use all kinds of creative ways to speak into our current life situations as we read His Word, the Bible. Hebrew 4:12 says,

"For the word of God is living and active. Sharper than any double-edged sword, it penetrates even to dividing soul and spirit, joints and marrow; it judges the thoughts and attitudes of the heart." Reading and understanding your Bible will not only deepen your relationship with God, but it will be one of the most important ways you filter out God's whispers from other voices in your life. If you hear a whisper from God that does not line up with the teaching of the Bible, it is not God. (There is a detailed discussion of this important topic coming in chapters nine and 10.) Finally, the Bible points us to Jesus and invites us into a relationship with Him through the Holy Spirit where it is possible to hear His voice more intimately in our daily lives.

Try it yourself. Ask God in your own words to speak louder to you as you read His written word, the Bible. Invite the Holy Spirit to guide you to specific passages as you read the Bible.

GOD, PLEASE WHISPER TO ME NOW...

Have you ever read the Bible and experienced hearing God through the passage you read?

Read 1 Kings, Chapter 19. Reflect on Elijah's faith-filled moments and his moments of despair. How does the Elijah story speak to you?

PRAYER

Lord, give me faith like Elijah, who the Bible claims is an imperfect, ordinary person just like me, but who also was a mighty man who had faith in God and heard God whisper directly to him. Amen.

.

5

Our God's Not Dead! He's Really Alive!

My message and my preaching were not with wise and persuasive words, but with a demonstration of the Spirit's power.
The Apostle Paul, 1 Corinthians 2:4

We can get by in life with a God who does not speak. Many at least think they do. But it is not much of a life, and it is certainly not the life that God intends for us.
Dallas Willard, Hearing God

My friend Michelle was diagnosed with Multiple Sclerosis four years ago. At the time, she had a five-year-old and was pregnant with their second little girl. Understandably, she was terrified. After the diagnosis, she felt like she was losing her mind and anxiety was taking over. She was having trouble just getting out of bed each day, and a terrible fear gripped her heart that made her feel paralyzed. Michelle would describe herself as a lapsed Catholic, but still had faith in God. She knew a lot about religion but very little about Jesus. She prayed daily but still found herself paralyzed by fear.

One day, she could barely make it into the shower because of the pain in her body, and she cried out to God, asking Him to take over her life. That night something unusual happened, which she says changed her view of God forever. As she say down in bed, suddenly,

"It was as if a peaceful Presence that I'd never before felt washed over me, and I just stood there never wanting to leave. When the experience of the Presence was gone, I was left feeling peaceful and unafraid. I knew it was God." Later, Michelle went to talk to a pastor about her experience: "It was then that I understood it was truly Jesus, through the Holy Spirit, that I was experiencing. When God came to me in that way, He healed me of the worst part of my diagnosis: He removed my fear of the disease, and I haven't been afraid since that day four years ago."

One of things I love about Michelle is her experience of the Holy Spirit. Her encounter with the Holy Spirit was not unlike the normal spiritual experience of those in the book of Acts. Like the people of the early church, Michelle's first direct experience of Jesus happened not through preaching, teaching, or intellectual truths about God. Instead, her first experience of Jesus was through a loving demonstration of the Spirit's power, which brought her healing and peace.

This was pretty much the norm for the believers in the New Testament. They first experienced Jesus by the Spirit showing up in acts of healing, power, and miracles, and later they would learn the theology behind their experience. Their intellect caught up with their experience after the fact.

Today, the norm seems very much the reverse of the experience of the church in Acts. In many Western churches, there is a greater emphasis and teaching on God, the Father and on our Savior, Jesus. There also seems to be more emphasis on the written Word, the Bible, good preaching, and Bible study. And yet, when it comes to teaching on and experiencing the Holy Spirit, we are weak in our coverage. Consequently, as Christians we often are strong in the Word, but our understanding of the Spirit is atrophied, weakened by its neglect.

As Corey, my teenager, and her friends exclaim at the top of their lungs (while riding down the highway, joining in with Michael Tait of the Newsboys),

"Our God's not dead! He's surely alive!" This lyric is true: He is alive. Jesus is not some dead guy that we worship. Christianity is unique in this belief. We do not worship a God who was once alive, but now dead, leaving behind only stagnant religious principles. Instead, we worship the Living God, Jesus Christ, who can be known in the here and now, present with us always through the Holy Spirit, who we can know and experience in our everyday life.

Who is the God who is whispering?

We cannot understand how God whispers without understanding the Holy Spirit. Frankly, the Holy Spirit has gotten a bad rap, and some Christians now see the Holy Spirit as some weird force or a just-for-the-fringe element.

I remember when my daughter, Annie, summed up some of the fears I hear most when it comes to the Holy Spirit. She was just four years old when she asked me some really funny questions about this Holy Spirit character. We were driving to school through the neighborhood, and I started to pray for her day, which is our typical morning's routine. For some reason, that morning, I prayed something she had apparently never heard before,

"Lord, please go with Annie to school. Be with her on the playground, and cover her with a blanket of your Holy Spirit so that she doesn't feel alone." After I had finished praying, Annie said flatly,

"Mom, I didn't know that Jesus had a blanket?" I laughed out loud.

"No, Annie," I said, "Jesus doesn't have a blanket. Then again, maybe He does. What I meant, though, when I asked Jesus to 'cover you with the blanket of the Holy Spirit,' is that He would go with you to school and surround you with His presence so you'd be safe." Annie was quiet a minute, and then she said, "Mom, is the Holy Spirit a good spirit or a bad spirit?"

Wow! It was such a wonderful, child-like question. There is nothing like a question from a four-year-old that makes you re-think how you are talking about God. That morning's routine drive to elementary school included a very out-of-the-ordinary theological discussion. I told Annie the Bible teaches that the Holy Spirit is the very presence of Jesus, which is a very, very good thing, and He is here so that she would know that Jesus is always with her. Even if she could not see Jesus, He was with her through the Holy Spirit. Then Annie, my little deep thinker, said,

"You mean the Holy Spirit is more powerful than Daddy?" I smiled,

"Yes, Annie, more powerful than Daddy." She was quiet again.

"Mom, can I ask the Holy Spirit to send away monsters and bad guys?" I smiled again at the innocence of her faith,

"Oh definitely. Annie, the Holy Spirit is way more powerful than any silly monster, and you can absolutely ask the Holy Spirit to protect you from bad guys." We got to school; Annie jumped out of the car, grabbed her backpack and shouted back at me before she walked onto the playground,

"Thanks, Mom! God is pretty cool to send the Holy Spirit to protect us!" With that, she bounded into the sea of three-foot tall Kindergartners.

Annie is a pretty wise kid, and that morning she asked questions that many Christians have struggled over for centuries. Christians are confused about the Holy Spirit, this mysterious member of the Trinity, and are unclear on His role in their lives. The Holy Spirit is not some mysterious, weird thing reserved for fringe folks. When Jesus was getting ready to leave this earth, He made it very clear that the Holy Spirit would come to us, to teach us, and to be the very near presence of God, always with us.

Not only does God want you to be intimately familiar with Jesus and His Word, but He also wants you to know His Spirit. Ben and I have a saying in our ministry that applies here: You can be filled with the Spirit and not be weird." Experiencing the presence of the Holy Spirit is absolutely possible for the normal, everyday Christian. The Holy Spirit is not a special icing on the cake reserved just for the "heavies" or the especially-gifted folks in prayer. It is not just for those who call themselves "charismatic," but for every Christian. I believe God meets us where we are, knows us as He made us, and desires that daily experiences with the Holy Spirit be a part of every Christian's walk with God.

The Spirit-Filled Life

Recently, I was teaching a conference in the East Bay on the Holy Spirit. An older gentleman in attendance approached me and asked plainly,

"Christy, I hear lots of talk about the Holy Spirit. When I was a kid, my pastor always talked about the Holy Ghost. All I knew was I didn't want to be anywhere near that Holy Ghost character, so I decided to focus on my Bible and preaching. What does being filled with the Spirit even look like?" After considering his question, I have come up with a general definition of what I believe being filled with the Holy Spirit looks like: It is being in an intimate relationship with Jesus, the Living God, where you learn to hear His voice, experience His very near Presence, and move in the spiritual power He promised his disciples.

My friend, Sharon, lives daily in this Spirit-filled life, and she hears God more than most people I have ever met. When I was eight months pregnant with Annie, I was a pastor at Menlo Park Presbyterian Church. One day, Sharon showed up at my door, and when I opened the door she blurted out,

"God has told me that He's going to start speaking to you in dreams, so here are some good books on hearing God in dreams." She shoved the books into my hands without question or doubt. My response was to laugh out loud. I did not think much about it after I had put the books aside, but I went to bed that night, and sure enough, had a dream. In the dream, my friend Scott came to me and said,

"Christy, I have a plan to revive the Presbyterian church." As is my usual response, I laughed at Scott in the dream, but then I started planning with him about how it would happen. All at once, we looked at one another and said together,

"The ministry will be called The Eagles Nest." After such a clear and profound dream, I woke up thinking, *Sharon is right as usual! But what the heck do I do with that?* I got out those books and started reading. My friend in the dream, Scott, had moved to Seattle, so the next time he came down to visit, we met for coffee. The dream was profound enough to move me to share the dream (but all the while secretly hoping then to be done with my job of handing off the prophetic word to him), so I told him,

"Scott, here is the dream I had, and I think it's a message for you and your ministry in the Presbyterian Church." When I was done delivering my hit- and-run message, he smiled and responded,

"Christy, I hate to tell you this, but I don't think that's a dream for me. I think it's about a ministry you are called to start about how people experience the Spirit of God. I'm only in the dream because I believe in you and your prophetic gifts of hearing God."

A year after that Pete's Coffee meeting with Scott, we launched Eagles Nest ministry. It is a "School of the Spirit" where we teach, equip, and empower believers in the Holy Spirit's ministry. We minister in hospitals, conferences, retreats, and churches. Our mission is to help ordinary people move in the Holy Spirit's power and hear God, pray for healing and learn to intercede for others.

In Spirit *and* in Truth

In Sharon's later interpretation of the dream, I represented the Spirit and

Scott represented the Word. Real revival comes to people who are strong in both the Word and the Spirit. We need to be a people who have well-developed muscles in both the Word and the Spirit. Otherwise, we will become imbalanced. If a believer is strong in only the Spirit, there is a danger of straying away from biblical guidelines and being swayed merely by emotions and imaginations. This was exactly the case with the Corinthian church in the Bible. The spiritual gifts were evident in power, but things got out of control, and people started hurting each other and the church.

At the Honolulu Convention Center, I was speaking on hearing God's voice. A lovely lady came to me and confessed,

"Christy, every time I think about trying to hear God more in my life, I'm drawn to that Corinthian church and how messy it got when people started trying to hear God's voice." Her honest inquiry ended with, "Isn't it safer to not experiment with these spiritual gifts? The apostle Paul had to rebuke those Corinthians for that stuff." My gentle response was,

"Actually, the Corinthian church is the perfect example of why we should not give up on spiritual gifts and hearing God." She looked puzzled. "You are right that Paul had to step in and correct them, but isn't it great that in the messiest church of all, when it came to the ministry of the Holy Spirit, Paul encourages them to keep going!" Paul wrote, "Follow the way of love, and eagerly desire the spiritual gifts, especially the gift of prophecy" (1 Corinthians 14:1). At the same time, the Bible tells us we are told to examine those prophetic words, or to "test the spirits, to see whether they are from God" (1 John 4:1).

We are not talking about hearing just any voice. We are not even talking about the power of positive thinking or talking to ourselves. We are talking about hearing the very real voice of the Living God. We are talking about the God of the Bible described as Emmanuel, God with us. He promised to still be with us after He rose from the dead and went to be with the Father in Heaven because He would come to us through the Holy Spirit. In Romans 8:9-11, "The Spirit," "Spirit of God," and "Spirit of Christ" are used as synonyms, interchangeable terms.

The Holy Spirit is the Spirit of Jesus. In essence, we are talking about learning what it means to be in a deeper relationship with Jesus through the

Holy Spirit where we learn to hear His whispering voice. It is not that complicated, but we sure make it seem that way for some strange reason. It is the Lord who initiates this communication with us. We do not make up this conversation on our own. Nothing makes me sadder that seeing Christians shrink back from the ministry of the Holy Spirit.

I believe that the sadness deep in my heart is a piece of God's heart when He sees His children afraid of experiencing all the gifts of His Holy Spirit. Jesus said, "I have come that they might have life, and have it to the full" (John 10:10). I am convinced that the abundant life includes a deep, personal, experiential relationship with Jesus, through the Holy Spirit.

One of the best pictures of humility when it comes to the Holy Spirit is found in the book of Acts, chapter 18. The passage is about how two humble people took Apollos under their care, to disciple him in the Holy Spirit. What is fascinating is that Apollos was already an amazing man of God. We are told he is a believer who "He had been instructed in the way of the Lord, and spoke with great fervor and taught about the Lord accurately, though he only knew the baptism of John" (Acts 18:25).

It is clear from the Bible that Apollos knew the Word of God well and was a powerful preacher. But there was something He was missing, and he knew it. His humility and yearning to experience all of God led him to Priscilla and Aquila, who the Bible tells us, "explained the way of God to him more adequately" (Acts 18:26). We know that Apollos stayed at their home, and they shared all they had experienced of the Holy Spirit.

Studying this passage in the original Greek language is very interesting. While different scholars wonder just what Priscilla and Aquila taught Apollos that he did not already know, it is important to note that these two believers (a husband and wife) were disciples of Paul. They did not have theological expertise or knowledge at the level of Apollos, but clearly they had something he did not. I think that Priscilla and Aquila put loving arms around Apollos, and helped him unwrap the gifts that the Spirit of God wanted him to have. Interestingly, the Bible points out that Apollos had the baptism of John (the water baptism of becoming a believer in Jesus) but not of the Spirit.

In the story of Priscilla and Aquila, there was a humble approach to teaching on who the Spirit is and how He moves. Contrast that with what I

GOD IS WHISPERING TO YOU

would call some not-so-helpful approaches regarding the Holy Spirit. Let me be crystal clear that, as a "theological mutt," I have been a pastor in both churches people would call charismatic as well as in churches that people would call *anti*-charismatic. I have made up my mind not to put myself in either camp. Instead, I want to be in the Apollos, Priscilla, and Aquila camp: embracing more of the Holy Spirit while preaching the Word of God with accuracy and fervor.

My husband is from the South and has what our congregation says is the gift of "Ben-isms." Ben, apparently, has the gift of capturing things in a phrase that makes people laugh, but which also sums up the situation pretty well. When it comes to the Holy Spirit and leaders claiming that God moves this way and not that way, Ben responds so wisely with,

"When it comes to the Holy Spirit, most folks seem to be either 'Latin' or 'German' in their approach." He says, "The Latins jump right in and experience the Holy Spirit, then understand it afterward. The Germans first understand the Spirit intellectually and theologically and then experience the Holy Spirit afterward." Neither approach is wrong, just different. I would add, however, that the New Testament Christians were more "Latin" in their Holy Spirit experiences. Typically, the early Christians had experiences with the Holy Spirit of healing, miracles or hearing God's voice, and then the disciples explained the theology of what they experienced afterward.

Another "Ben-ism" he often says is,

"God is the 600 pound Gorilla! He can move any way He wants!" I love this saying when it comes to hearing God's whispers and the ministry of the Holy Spirit. We get into trouble when we limit the ways God can speak, as if we could ever do that. Jesus is infinitely creative in the ways He whispers through the Spirit. The key question we need to wrestle with is this: Are we open to more of God and experiencing Him through the Holy Spirit?

In fact, my own experience of "Washington, D.C., Chapter One" versus "Washington, D.C., Chapter Two" is a great example of the difference between an intellectual understanding of God through the Bible and sermons, and the addition of a Spirit-empowered ministry. "Washington, D.C., Chapter One" snapshot: I am flying to five cities a day, eating 27 chickens a month, and having a "Help, God!" prayer life while crying on my shower floor.

I was a little like Apollos in that I knew my Bible, went to church, but on the inside was exhausted and longing for more. "Washington, D.C., Book Two" snapshot: I experienced the "more" of the Holy Spirit I always longed for but did not even know it. God had blown away every intellectual box I had put Him in. He showed me that He was still in the business of miracles, that He still whispered to people, and that He loved me more than I could ever have imagined.

When my kids get home from school, I cannot wait to hear about their days. I make them their favorite snack and then listen to whatever is on their hearts. Corey is my teenager, and I get to hear all of the boy drama and all about the endlessly wide world of texting that is on her heart. It is a privilege to listen to and to love her. Annie is my wise middle school kid, who has already authored her own children's book. She inspires me and says things that I just know are from God's heart. Benji is all boy, but still a blond, blue-eyed, adorable third- grader who says these hilarious things that bring me so much joy. Each of my kids is different, with different things needed from me.

It is the same way with Jesus. He loves us all the same, and He knows us fully and completely. Jesus knows the "more" you need when it comes to experiencing the Holy Spirit and God's whispering voice in your life. God especially longs to pour out his "more" into our lives so that we can face the hard things in our lives.

As we finish this chapter, I want to invite you to consider your relationship with the Holy Spirit. It does not matter whether you have had a lot of experience with the Holy Spirit or very little at all. It does not matter whether you have had good experiences with the ministry of the Holy Spirit or bad ones. The only question is simply this: Do you long to experience the Holy Spirit more in your life? I want to encourage you that praying for "more" is always a safe prayer to pray. God knows you like no one else. He knows exactly what "more" you need to grow closer to Him and to hear His whispering voice louder in your life.

This past year, I was invited to preach on healing at Peninsula Covenant Church in Redwood City, CA. Shortly after my sermon, I got a call from a woman who ministers at the Veteran's Hospital in Palo Alto. She told me about a young man I'll call Adam, who had recently been hit by a bomb in Afghanistan, and was completely paralyzed. His wife had asked us to come and pray.

When I entered the room, my heart sank looking at Adam and his wife, who was sitting quietly by his bedside, holding his hand. She told me the story of the improvised explosive device (IED) going off and how he had been flown from Afghanistan to Germany to Bethesda and now to Palo Alto. They were getting ready to move him again, and there had been little healing progress. As I stood by Adam, I looked into his eyes, and it was clear that he could understand every word. It was as if he was a prisoner in his own body: present and yet unable to talk or move.

I cannot imagine a harder life, and he and his wife are forever etched in my mind as modern-day heroes. We prayed for his healing and for encouragement. As I was finishing our prayer, I heard God whisper, *Dad.* It was such a quiet whisper that I almost did not share it. But, I thought if there is anything in this whisper expressly for Adam that would encourage him, I had better share it. So, I mustered up all my courage and said,

"Adam, as I pray, I keep hearing the word, 'dad'? I'm not sure if that means anything to you. I know you are a father, but possibly Jesus might be trying to show you something, so I wanted you to know." Tears began to run down Adam's face. Surprised, I looked at his wife, and she knew immediately what was going on. She looked down at him and said,

"Honey, you miss your dad, right?" She told me that Adam and his father have an especially close relationship, and that he was worried because they just got word his dad had an early diagnosis of Alzheimer's. She told Adam, "I'll call your dad, and we'll see if we can get him down here soon, baby."

Two weeks later, we were invited to a Purple Heart ceremony for Adam. His dad was there. Before Adam came out for his purple heart, I had the opportunity to go and talk with Adam's dad. I shared with him the whisper of the Holy Spirit that I heard while praying a few weeks before he came down. Tears ran down the father's face and he said,

"I'm so thankful you told me that. Sometimes I wonder if God really sees what's going on. We've always tried to raise Adam to know about God, and it helps me so much to know God knows."

The Holy Spirit is the very real presence of the Living God who comforts us, speaks words of encouragement to us, and breathes new life to us when we wonder if God is real or not. It is true. In the words of that *Newsboys* song always blaring in our house: "Our God's not dead! He's surely alive!"

GOD, PLEASE WHISPER TO ME NOW...

Read the story of Apollos and his experience of the Holy Spirit in Acts chapter 18.

When it comes to hearing God's whispers and the Holy Spirit, do you take a more intellectual or experiential approach? How can you just be yourself and still grow in hearing the Lord speak more in your life?

What does "more" look like to you when it comes to experiencing God whispering and the Holy Spirit?

PRAYER

Jesus, I need more of you. Lord, you know me like no one else. You know my hopes and fears when it comes to asking You to speak more into my life. Please, remove all barriers, all blocks so that I can embrace this gift you long for me to have. God, give me a heart like Apollos. Help me to be humble and to be open to new experiences with You. I want to be a person who is open to more of the Holy Spirit. Jesus, I want to experience the abundant life you promised. Pour out your Spirit and your gifts into my life so that I can grow in hearing your voice and also glorify you more. Amen.

6

God's Loudest Whisper

And I pray that you, being rooted and established in love, may have power, together with all the saints, to grasp how wide and long and high and deep is the love of Christ, and to know this love which surpasses knowledge—that you may be filled in all measure of all the fullness of God.
Ephesians 3:19

There is nothing that ordinary souls need more than the scriptural enablement to believe that God is, indeed, with them and loves them.
Leanne Payne, *The Healing Presence*

Years ago, Ben talked me into going to India to minister to the untouchables, one of the poorest people groups on earth. I am embarrassed to admit that I did not want to go. You have to understand this about me: I do not even like camping. I do not really like travelling, especially on 15-hour flights, into places that are dirty and dusty, where I might get sick. Honestly, I am the kind of person who can pick up a parasite getting a drink of water on the playground, so the idea of hanging out where the water is possibly the most contaminated in the world, well, scared me.

But God had other plans for me. Ben and I flew to India, unknowingly journeying to an experience of God's love that would shape the rest of my life. One memory is etched in my mind forever.

On the plane flying in, Ben explained me to what we were about to witness.

He told me about the untouchables, a people group in India that the government claims number about 169 million. You may think that since Gandhi came to India, "untouchability" was supposed to be destroyed. Everyone who lives in India knows this just is not true. The fact is, it is hard to change a paradigm that has been around for thousands of years.

In India, an untouchable person is expected to know their place in life. That means they are not only poor, but they are the modern-day lepers we picture in the Bible, untouchable, unclean, unsafe. Untouchables have a life-long job of carrying dead bodies and cleaning the latrines. They live on the open sewers of India, sleeping alongside the pigs. Walking the streets of India, if you were to see one of the untouchables, you would not know it by his or her size or color; you would know his position in the caste by how he reacts to you. An untouchable would cover his head in shame and erase his footprints near you, for he is taught that his touch defiles other people. He is of less worth than animals.

In fact, if an untouchable tries to enter a Hindu temple or Muslim mosque, he or she risks death. It is a horrible life of unimaginable suffering and shame that few of us have ever encountered. God has been doing a powerful work among the untouchables, though, and our friend, Philip Prasad and his wife, Elizabeth, run a ministry that has led well over a million people to Christ in the past 20 years alone.

The first day of our trip to India, we rode in a bouncy Jeep through the dusty streets of India, over ditches in the road and alongside people on bicycles or donkeys. It was crazy. We entered the first village where we were to meet the untouchables, and Philip told me a pastor had been there for about six weeks telling people about Jesus.

Pulling up to our stop, a drove of pigs scattered to make way for the Jeep; I could see the open sewers flowing with human waste. I closed my eyes and asked Jesus to help me reach out to people in such poverty. My heart burdened by the background of stench and poverty, I was blown away with what I saw when I climbed out of the Jeep: Children were rushing to greet us, with joy and huge smiles on their faces as they shouted to us,

"Jai Masih Ki! Jai Masih Ki!" a saying that means, "Victory to Jesus!" Several little children grabbed our hands and began to pull us into their humble little huts along the open sewer banks. We sat down on dirt floors, and they began to sing,

"For thousands of years, the Hindus have made us dance like monkeys, but Jesus has come and given us new life." I could only stare in awe at the clearest picture of transformation I had ever seen, with these faces of joy before me, dirty pigs and rivers of human waste behind them. After they stopped singing, Philip stood up and said,

"And now, Christy will preach the Word of God to us." I was stunned. He did not warn me ahead of time that I would be speaking, and I was frankly so overwhelmed with the faith of these untouchable people, that I felt completely unworthy to speak anything to them. So, I stood up, and looked out at these dear people, and said the first thing that came to my mind,

"Jesus came to a village much like yours, and He said, 'Let the little children come to me.'" I paused, gaining composure, "Do you know why Jesus said that?" I did not expect an answer at all, and was planning to continue, but a little boy in the back, about nine years old, raised his hand.

Everyone was surprised and turned to stare at this little boy. Philip motioned for him to stand up. He stood up tall in front of his village with his dirt-stained legs and bare feet, looked me straight in the eye, and said in a proud, bold voice,

"Jesus said, 'Let the little children come to me' because to us belongs the Kingdom of heaven!" Tears began to stream down my face, and I sat down, unable to go on. (Thankfully, Philip took over the preaching from there!) No matter where I travel, what God has for me, I know I will never, ever forget that little boy.

The love of Jesus radiated from his face in the most pure, powerful way I had ever seen. Even though he had only known Jesus a few short weeks, he had hold of the Truth. He knew that Jesus, the Creator of the Universe, loved him, an untouchable, with a love stronger than the oppressive caste system that defined him, deeper than the identity of trash that branded him, wider than the reaches of his poverty, and longer than the span of hardship and struggle he was sure to face.

Do you have any idea how much God loves you? Whatever your personal experience of God's love is so far in your life, I can promise you this: God loves you more than you have ever experienced or imagined. His love for you is real. It is deeper and bigger than your wildest dreams. His love is able to overcome any obstacles you face in life. More than any other thing God wants to say to you, He wants you to hear his loud call, *I am with you. I am for you. I am trying to get through to you how much I adore you.*

The problem is that no matter how much we have heard people tell us, "God loves you," we do not always believe it. In fact, we hardly ever believe it. Oh yeah, I know, we might believe it intellectually. We might even preach about it. We might believe in the love of God for our friends, family, or neighbors, but not for us. Not really. We constantly underestimate the love of God for us, personally, and we rarely experience the biblical truth of His love for us in a life-changing way. My friend, Jordan Seng, has this funny way He speaks on this truth. He always starts by saying,

"Before I begin speaking, there is something you need to know about me." Then he pauses, and with a smile on his face, says, "I'm God's favorite person. You might be God's second favorite person, but I'm really His favorite." His point is simple: When we understand and believe in this identity, we are unstoppable.

When Benji was a toddler, I would strap him into his car seat, kiss him on the forehead, and with a twinkle in my eye, ask him this question:

"Benj, who is Mom's special boy?" He would get a big smile on his face and nearly scream with joy,

"ME!" Today, Benji is eight. I keep asking him that question, over and over again: Who is Mom's special boy? As an eight-year-old, he does not want to be so bold as to scream out "Me!" anymore (that would be too silly for a cool third grader). But he will still smile slyly, and say, "It's me, Mom. I'm your special boy." I will never stop asking Benji that question, no matter how old he gets, because as long as I am alive, he needs to know that he is special and precious to me forever. He needs to know how much I love him.

Benji is named after my husband, Ben, who is the love of my life. Ben and I met and fell in love at Fuller Theological Seminary where we were both studying to become pastors. The Lord truly rescued me by bringing Ben into my life as my soul mate and partner. I can still wake up in a cold sweat thinking about what would have happened if I had married some of the men I used to date. The truth is that I can be stubborn and think I know the best path for my life.

Thankfully, God loves me enough to break into my life and speak His whispers of love even when I do not come close to deserving it. On a mission trip to Africa, this became painfully clear. Single at the time, I went on the trip with my boyfriend and a group of people leading a conference on prayer ministry. Emotionally, I was tired of the single life and thought this boyfriend and I were great together. He was a pastor; I wanted to go into ministry. What could be better? Right? Wrong.

The problem was this was a painful relationship and this man cheated on me regularly. There was this pattern of love then rejection in a lot of my relationships, and this one was no different. The problem was I could not let go of it for fear of living life alone. Looking back, I realize now that deep down I did not think I deserved more. Letting go of him felt impossible—until God spoke truth.

At this particular conference, I was in a worship service. As I was singing I looked over at my boyfriend, and I heard God whisper to me something heartbreaking and yet freeing, *Christy, I have far better things in mind for you than this.* It was as if someone had stabbed me in the heart. I knew it was true. I wish I could say I broke up with him immediately in obedience to God's whisper. No way. (Remember, I am very stubborn?)

Instead, it took many more months of getting more and more beaten down, of God letting me experience the reality staying in that relationship, of trusting that God was enough, before finally taking a step of faith to say goodbye and let go There is a verse in Jonah that has been a theme verse in my life: "Those who cling to worthless idols forfeit the grace that could be theirs" (Jonah 3:2).

I realized that I was holding onto this man's view of me, so wanting his love that I was unwilling to obey God and let him go. As the song goes, I was "looking for love in all the wrong places." I do not know your story, but in my life, God constantly has to pry my fingers off different idols so that I can experience the full depth of the love that only He can give me. Not long after that realization, I was in a worship service and something strange happened: I had a picture of myself pop into my head that changed my life and began this journey of healing my very broken self-image. The picture got clearer and clearer, and as I was worshipping, I saw myself in a white bridal gown, with a crown of flowers upon my head. My face was radiant with joy. Then I heard Jesus whisper loudly in my head saying, *Turn to Psalm 45.*

Moved by the Spirit, I sat down right there and opened my Bible to these words: "Listen daughter, consider and give ear. Forget your people and your father's house. The King is enthralled with your beauty, honor Him for He is your Lord" (Psalm 45:10-11).

Tears began to run down my face. For the first time, I realized that most of my life I had been believing all these lies about me, all those lies spoken by others who loved me conditionally, imperfectly, selfishly. But the truth was that God loved me. This was how He saw me. In that moment, God began sinking into my heart how much He loved me.

I started to grasp the beauty of the truth that Jesus could be my husband in this time of loneliness. Not long after that, I met Ben. If God had not pried my hands off my idol of needing to choose my own path and my mate, I would have been choosing less than what He had for me. Do not misunderstand me: I do not believe the man I "let go of" was a bad person. It is simply that God's ways are better than ours. God loved me enough to speak loudly into my life that He had another plan, and His whispers of love set me free to marry the man that He intended for my life.

When you hear God whispering messages of love to your heart, all of life is changed. You have power to overcome the big problems you face because you know, not just in your head but in your heart, that God loves more than you ever understood before. The love of God, not just for others, not just the "For God so loved the world" love, and not even the love you hear about in a good sermon, but a love that conveys how head over heels he is for us, one that transforms lives.

The love of God becomes real, not just intellectually, but deep inside the soul. None of us can fully comprehend it. There is always more. In the words of Ephesians, Jesus wants us to grasp "how wide and long and high and deep is the love of Christ" (3:18). And here is the kicker: He wants us to know this love that surpasses knowledge. It is not just head knowledge that God wants us to have. It is a deep, heart-level experience that the God of the Universe is head over heels in love with us.

When that happens, we have more strength to fight life's battles. We can then operate from a place of safety and in a cocoon of love, knowing that God is with us. Somehow the things that are causing us stress and pain in this life begin to dim as we are caught up in the truth that the God of the Universe delights over us.

When I moved from Washington, D.C. to Pasadena, California to attend Fuller Theological Seminary, I went into culture shock. I know that sounds kind of silly. It certainly was not as extreme of culture shock like my later trip to India would be, but for me, California was a different world from my Washingtonian life. I was used to people in business suits, high heels and power lunches on Capitol Hill. The first morning I woke up in my new apartment on the Fuller Seminary campus, I opened my windows and saw students walking around in shorts and flip-flops. I looked up at the trees and remember saying out loud,

"I hate palm trees." I had left behind one identity and was trying to embrace a new life. I was still on the government payroll, travelling with Mrs. Dole, but also working as a teaching assistant, trying to make new friends and attending school full time. I would come home to the most eclectic assortment of messages on my voicemail: the professor needing me to grade papers, the Labor Department in D.C. telling me about an upcoming trip they needed me to advance, the California Highway Patrol connecting with me so I could coordinate the visit, a new friend from Hebrew class who wanted coffee.

I was split in so many directions that I was facing a pseudo-identity crisis, wondering, *Who am I, anyway*? Ever feel that way? When you seek the identity that God speaks about you, you hear this: You are my beloved child. In Romans 8:14-17, God says this about those who put their faith in Jesus:

For all those who are led by the Spirit of God are children of God. For you did not receive a spirit of slavery to fall back into fear, but you have received a spirit of adoption. When we cry, "Abba! Father!" it is that very Spirit bearing witness with our spirit that we are children of God. (NRSV)

Kids seem to accept this biblical truth way easier than adults. I was reading this passage to Annie, and she said in the matter-of-fact way Annie does,

"Cool. I didn't really get that I was God's princess." Annie was so right. That was exactly how God views her. It is exactly how God views you! As a child of the King, you are God's prince or princess.

All of life would be different if we really, truly grasped how much God loves us and that we are not alone. When the reality of God's incredible love penetrates our doubts and fears, and takes root in our soul, we are filled with an "I can" attitude, instead of the "I can't" one.

For when you know that He is with you, He loves you, you really can do "all things through [Christ] who gives me strength" (Philippians 4:13). More than any other message God wants to get through, not just to your head, but also to your heart, is how much He loves you. In fact, I think that is the whole reason the Lord made it possible to hear the whispering voice of God through the Holy Spirit! Life is dang hard enough. The Lord knew we would face pain after pain, and so many voices that would batter us down. When we grasp how much God loves us, we are set free from the earplugs we talked about in chapter three. We are no longer bound up by fear, pain, and disbelief when the God of all creation breaks into our world with a shout of His love into our daily life.

Through the Holy Spirit, we can actually hear God's whispering voice in a way that penetrates our hearts, so that we can exclaim, "God is real. He is here, and I never knew He loved me that much!"

After I had my third child, I went through a deep depression. I was recovering from my third C-section, with a two-year-old and four-year-old at home. In the midst of all this, God was calling us to leave the safe, comfortable job at a large church in order to plant New Hope Peninsula Church. All that meant finding a new place to live, not knowing where our income or health insurance would come from, not knowing where my kids would go to school. It was all overwhelming.

Every day, I kept calling out to God, saying, *Lord, where are you?! God, you picked the wrong person to do this!* By far, the worst part was that I felt like a terrible mom. Crying all the time, being irritable and generally exhausted was my daily reality. One day, my husband said,

"That's it! I'm taking the kids today and dropping you off at a church so you can worship alone, where no one knows you!" I got myself a Starbucks and stumbled into a local church, sat in the back row, tears streaming down my face. As we were worshipping, I experienced God speaking to me in a way that I could not possibly doubt it was Him. I was lamenting how pitiful I was, and I heard the Lord say to me, *Christy, this is how I see you.* Then, a very faint picture came into my mind in the distance. It was blurry, but I closed my eyes and asked Jesus to make it clearer if it was really from Him. The picture got clearer as I saw that this person in the picture was me.

As I peered into this picture, I saw this banner over me with the words "Mother of the Year" written across it. I could not stop crying. Complete strangers kept handing me Kleenex asking if I was OK. Yes, I was OK. I was better than OK because God was speaking to the negative, self-loathing view of myself by showing me His view of me instead. Of course, I knew I was not close to a perfect mom! I am just a broken person who God has put His hand upon. Jesus knew just what to say to get through to my heart. Somehow, I left that sanctuary different on the inside, knowing that He was with me and I would somehow be able to face my life challenges.

Do you know you who are?

God is saying to you, *You are my child. You are deeply loved and I know every worry, dream, and desire in your heart.* I love the passage in the Bible that reminds us that because of Jesus, because we are God's kids, we have full permission to climb up onto His lap and talk to Him anytime we want. He longs for us to do this!

> *Therefore, since we have a great high priest who has gone through the heavens, Jesus the Son of God, let us hold firmly to the faith we profess. For we do not have a high priest who is unable to sympathize with our weaknesses, but we have one who has been tempted in every way, just as we are—yet was without sin. Let us then approach the throne of grace with confidence, so that we may receive mercy and find grace to help us in our time of need. (Hebrews 4:14–16)*

A few years ago my husband Ben had to take a stand in a ministry he served that was unpopular with some of the people he cared about there. Some unpopular decisions are easier than others because there are definite, clear-cut moral or spiritual truths that guide the decision-making process. This, however, was not one of those times. His decision was one that was not popular even with those Ben respected and who respected him. The people who were disappointed in Ben were people whose opinions mattered to him, so their disapproval was deeply wounding.

It was one of those lonely moments with God—like when Noah began building a boat in the middle of the desert—where you do the right thing for the right reasons, but few people understand it. I have never been so proud of him.

Not long after that decision, I had a vision of Ben, and I shared it with him. In the vision, Ben was entering a party with many people there. Some were from the ministry and they did not welcome him. But just beyond the door of the party was a huge crowd of people, cheering, holding signs that said, "Way to go, Ben!" and "We love you, Ben!" As Ben entered the party, the crowd was standing, the applause deafening. In the crowd Abraham, Moses, Joshua, and Jesus cheered him on.

I was so excited to share this encouraging vision that I drove home as fast as I could without speeding and rushed in the door. I blurted out the vision and waited for his response. Ben was not impressed. In fact, his face looked sad, and he simply said.

"Wow, cool," in the most unimpressed way. I knew better than to press it further, so I just left him with that, asking God to show him if the vision was really from Him or not.

Several months later, Ben was on an airplane flying to a mission trip. The plane was ascending high over the Golden Gate Bridge, and he had fallen into a deep sleep, exhausted from the difficult path he had walked in recent months.

Suddenly, Ben woke up, startled, to the sound of loud applause. Confused, he looked around the airplane and noticed that everyone was quietly reading, with no one clapping at all. Immediately, God brought that vision into Ben's mind, and he could see all the people at the party cheering for him.

He could see Abraham, Moses, Joshua, and Jesus—all the same people that I saw in my vision. The presence of Jesus was so overpowering that Ben began to weep right there on the airplane flying in the clouds high over the San Francisco Bay.

I have only seen my husband cry twice in our lives together: once when his dad died and the other when Corey was born. But in that moment, as He experienced God's love, God's approval, and the truth of how His Father in heaven saw him, tears of joy poured down Ben's face. He heard the voice of God, saying, *Well done, good and faithful servant.* God's approval was the only one that really mattered.

Can you hear God clapping for you? Do you know that God is your biggest cheerleader? If you have never heard God's whispering voice of love, or wish that you could hear it more, I have some really great news for you. God knows how to get through to you how much He loves you. Your job is simply to be open and to ask God to speak clearly about how much He loves you. God is really good at that.

As we finish this chapter, I want to invite you to do a few things that I am hoping will help you in your own journey of hearing God's whispers of love. These exercises are designed to help you experience God's love more in your personal life. As much as you may think you understand the biblical truth about how God loves you, please know that we cannot possibly grasp the depths of His love.

When Jesus looks at you, the smile on His face shines because He loves you with an everlasting love. Ask the Holy Spirit to make the truth of that love very real to your heart. Lastly, I would invite you to pray this prayer: "Lord, give me eyes to see myself as YOU see me. Help me to truly experience your deep, personal love for me and to hear your voice. Amen."

GOD, PLEASE WHISPER TO ME NOW...

How much are you experiencing the truth of God's deep, radical love for you right now?
I invite you to try the short exercise below to help you find out how much you are experiencing God love at this point in your life. This is not about your intellectual knowledge of God's love, or your theological views about how much God loves you. This is about a heart-level experience of God's love right now. Remember that our experience of God's love will change often in our lifetime, depending on our circumstances and journey of faith. This exercise is designed to help you know where you are right now.

The private window into your view of God's love
Think of a big need in your life right now. Maybe it is a financial need or a new job. Maybe it is an area of your life where you need advice, but have no idea who can help. Possibly your struggle is at work, in your marriage or concerning your children. Maybe it is a painful relationship that needs restoration or a physical healing you long for and have prayed for and has not happened. Those are a few possibilities, but you fill in the blank. What is a big need in your life right now where you wish God would show up and speak? Write it down here.

My place of need:

Now, I want you to think about and write down two people. First, is "Person A": This is someone who, well, really bugs you! When you think of this person, you feel judged, mistrusted, or just bad about yourself when you are around them. Face it: You just do not like this person. You do not feel safe with this person. Write down that name. (Don't worry—you can scratch it out later!)

Person A:

Now, write down "Person B," someone who when you see, you smile. Perhaps it is a best friend or a family member. You feel completely safe around this person, like no matter what you say, he or she will not judge you but love you unconditionally. This is a person who makes you feel completely safe being yourself. If you do not have anyone that fits that description, just write down someone you admire or trust. Write down that name.

Person B:

Next, picture yourself walking into a coffee shop to meet Person A. Imagine sitting with them and how you would tell them about your big need. What would you say? Would you pour out your heart? Would you ask them for advice? Or would you just tell them a few things because you would not trust them with the whole problem? Would you even communicate with them at all? Would you just assume that they do not care about you so they are not safe to share such intimate problems with?

Then, imagine walking next door to another coffee shop, and as you walk inside, you see Person B. He or she is smiling at you, and rush up to give you a hug. You sit down at he or she goes to order your favorite drink, knowing what you like. Returning to the table, Person B says,

"Tell me what's going on? I can tell you are carrying something heavy. Is everything OK? How can I pray for you?"

How would you respond? What would come out of your mouth?

I am guessing that you would share at an entirely different level. You would pour out your heart, maybe cry, or ask for advice. Why? Because you would know that this person loves you and will not judge you. You respect his or her advice more than anyone else. This is a very different conversation, a completely opposite interaction from that with Person A.

Here is a harder question to ponder: When you think of sitting down to talk with Jesus, do you picture Him more like Person A or Person B? (By the way, this might not be how you felt a year ago, or a week ago. It is just how you feel right now.) There is a continuum below, and I would invite you to put an "x" by where you think where your perception of Jesus would then be when you read that question. What is important is not where you know it should be, but where it stands honestly at this moment. There is no right or wrong answer: It is simply an honest reflection about your experience of God's love for you right now.

Person A ——————————————————— Person B

    1   2   3   4   5   6   7   8   9   10

PRAYER

Lord, help me to understand, not just in my head, but deep in my heart, the truth of how much you love me. Open the eyes of my heart this week to a deeper understanding of your love. Help me to hear you whispering messages of love directly to me. I need to get this at a deeper level and only You can do it. I ask you for a breakthrough when it comes to experiencing your radical love for me. In Jesus' name, Amen.

7

Whispers in the Dark

The Lord is close to the brokenhearted and saves those who are crushed in spirit.
Psalm 34:18

Usually when God speaks, it's through a quiet whisper, but when we are in deep pain, it's as if He's shouting through a megaphone.
C.S. Lewis

Nobody can escape experiencing some dark times in this life. When we encounter suffering, mere head knowledge about God is not enough. We need a deep, experiential understanding that God is real and that we are not alone. One whisper from God in those painful times is like gold. More than ever, we need to hear God's whispering voice break through our dark clouds saying, *Do not be afraid, for I am right here with you. Cry out to me, and I will help you.*

One phone call can change your whole life. The "one phone call" I will never forget happened on a Sunday afternoon with everyone at home, except for Ben, who was riding his road bike. Ben was training for a big Century bike ride, so it was not unusual for him to be gone for several hours. Our home phone rang, and I heard my daughter, Corey, answer it. I could hear her voice from the other room, and she sounded scared, so I rushed in to find out why. She handed me the phone, her face white, and said,

"It's the Fire Department, and they say Daddy's been in a bike accident." My heart stopped, but I tried to act calm as I took the phone from her.

"Is this Christy Pierce?" a voice on the phone asked. "Ma'am, your husband was hit by a car on Edgewood Road and is in serious condition. He's been rushed by ambulance to the Stanford Emergency Room Trauma Center. You need to come down immediately."

As a pastor who prays for healing, I am very familiar with the Stanford emergency room. I know some of the doctors there by name and spend more time there than I would like. When I arrived, they claimed a "Ben Pierce" was not there, and I insisted that they were wrong. I explained that the paramedics had just called me and was starting to feel panicky when a doctor came out to find me.

"Mrs. Pierce? Your husband is here but was listed as a 'John Doe' when they rushed him in. I'm going to take you to him now. He's alive and awake, but in very serious condition," he paused, "Are you able to handle that?"

When I entered the emergency room, my breath caught in my throat. Ben was in what my prayer team refers to as "the bad room" (not that there are any "good rooms" in the E.R., but this was the severe trauma room where it is not uncommon to see people dead and covered with sheets). I rushed in, and Ben looked at me, blood running down his face, tears in his eyes. He began,

"I'm so sorry, honey. I'm so sorry." It was so typical of Ben, worried about me and my reaction, instead of his own well-being. We spent the night there with the trauma team doing CT scans and MRIs, eventually sewing up his face with 16 stitches on his forehead and treating the road rash. Friends from New Hope Peninsula Church were awesome, and they came down to stand with us and pray. Cindy was in the E.R. with me, wiping the blood from Ben's eyes when he needed it. Kim was there helping hold me together, and Rod came to pray. Sharon and Cynthia came to pray for healing. God was moving there in great power. The nurse who treated Ben's face, Chris, was a Christian. Seeing our gathering of believers, he told us,

"We have a lot of Christians working here tonight. How about I bring them over and pray with you guys?" Some of the Christian staff laid hands on Ben right there in the E.R. and prayed for him. I can tell you from years of experience in the trauma center that is just not something you see every day.

Finally, the doctor came in with good news, claiming that what happened was literally a miracle. Ben had fractured his neck in two places—both the C1 and C4 disks. The doctor explained,

"I can't begin to tell you how fortunate you are to be alive. Most patients who fracture the C1 disk don't usually survive. Forget about brain damage or being paralyzed, the C1 is at the base of the skull, which makes you a living, breathing miracle." We wept with gratitude to God. The doctor shared our joy, but also told us what we would soon find out for ourselves: This healing journey would be a very long road.

We came home a few days later, Ben's neck in a huge brace, stitches covering his face and severe road rash all over his body. The kids were in shock. I did not realize it because I was in full-on pastor mode, but I was too.

Just ten days before Ben's bike accident, Corey had taken a bad fall off a horse. Jumping over a fence, her horse suddenly stopped and Corey flew off, slamming her head into the barrier, leaving her with a severe concussion. Now, we had two family members with head trauma and post-concussive symptoms, which meant horrible headaches, vision problems, and fatigue. We are forever grateful for our New Hope Peninsula Church family during those weeks. Our neighbors were amazing in providing anything from meals to play dates for the kids. But that doctor had been right, it would be a very long road, and this was just beginning.

If ever there were a time to walk by faith in hardship, this was it for our family. Corey was not healing well. She valiantly tried to go back to school, but each day the headaches and vision blurring were so bad, she would need to come home. A few months later, we had to pull her out of school and start doing the lessons at home. She also developed an autoimmune disorder of some kind, which Stanford first diagnosed as Lyme Disease.

Corey was in chronic pain and became very depressed—understandable for a teenager in middle school, only wanting to be normal and to be at school with friends. Instead, she was home with blinding headaches, body aches, and severe fatigue. It was a lonely, isolating time of doctors, blood tests, MRIs, and sadness. One of the biggest losses was that she could no longer ride horses, a first love for her.

I, in the meantime, was pouring myself out for Ben and Corey, being the best nurse, wife, and mom I could manage, while also trying to keep a semblance of "normal life" going for Annie and Benji, who were also suffering from this family crisis. Ben and I tried to return to New Hope Peninsula Church, our small church plant, which was already struggling with the loss of their two pastors. We did not have a huge staff to delegate our ministry to, but some very faithful friends who valiantly kept the ship afloat in our absence.

Once Ben was back pastoring the church, it became painfully clear that he had returned to work too soon. I wish we knew then what we know now: Severe head trauma accidents of this level take years of recovery for most patients. We finally gave up and made the only choice possible: take medical leave and shut down the church. It was heartbreaking. For Ben, stepping down as pastor of New Hope Peninsula Church, which we birthed seven years before and had poured everything we had into, was devastating. Not to mention that we were now a family without income and uncertain what would happen to our future life and ministry.

Ben and I sought Jesus like never before. We both had our moments of crying out to God, *Why Lord?!* We had preached for 20 years the biblical truth that God is with us in times of suffering, and that we should rejoice in our trials, but it was a daily choice for our hearts to follow that truth. Corey, too, was at a crisis of faith and would frequently ask me,

"Mom, I don't understand God. We are a family of pastors, trying to do one of the hardest things in ministry, starting a new church in an area where people don't know Jesus. Mom, why, *why* would Jesus let this happen to us?" My heart was heavy and though I knew all the correct theological answers to her questions, they seemed like a limp response to a 10-year-old in chronic pain watching her family lose everything.

We clung to Jesus and prayed like crazy. We begged Him to help us see what He was doing in this hard time and how we should walk by faith. Then, Corey and I had an unexpected gift. A family friend, Victoria, heard God's whisper to give Corey two wild mustang foals to foster. Other friends came along side Corey to help her learn to raise and to train them. Those two beautiful horses were such a source of joy for us. Corey was praying to God constantly to help heal her and our family.

She carried the verse Romans 8:28 everywhere with her: "And we know that in all things, God works for the good of those who love him, who are called according to his purpose. God is able to work all things together for good for those who love Him." Pretty soon, God did some little miracles for Corey that would shape her faith forever.

Our friend Becky, who was helping her train the horses, had a vision for Corey to take Penny, the little filly, to Reno for a wild mustang taming show in front of hundreds of people. That process required Corey to raise $3,500, speak in front of large crowds, write newspaper articles, make a website, design products, and (did I not yet mention?) do the near-impossible task of training a wild mustang foal to ride five hours in a small trailer, then perform at the Reno Convention Center on television before hundreds of people. It was clearly the Lord's gift to our Corey, and we watched in awe as He answered the cries of a 10-year-old girl. As Becky said,

"If you can train a mustang foal, it's like the Olympics of the horse world, and you sure won't be afraid of many other things." It was an amazing chapter in our lives and of God, indeed, working good out of hardship for Corey and for our family. We are forever grateful to Kip and Becky, the Sommersets, Victoria and the many friends who walked alongside Corey to help make this dream become real for our 10-year-old daughter and this 10-month-old mustang foal.

But before the light of Corey's breakthrough could even dim, things took a turn for the worse again. A family trip to Tahoe was supposed to be fun and restful, as my extended family from Texas and Kansas came for a family reunion. The trip started out wonderfully. The nine cousins swam in the lake, riding big orange paddle boats and laughing together. It was peaceful and serene. I sat there in the sun on the warm, sandy beach, looking over the blue Tahoe water, and told my sister,

"You know, it's really been a hard couple of years, but things are getting better." I felt I was seeing the light at the end of our dark tunnel. But that night, Annie got very sick and started vomiting, with terrible headaches and abdominal pain. A local doctor diagnosed her with possible altitude sickness, and I had to leave with her immediately in order to get her down to sea level.

As we arrived home, I got sick too. As a mom with three young children, we have had about every virus and stomach flu you can get in the human petri dish that is preschool and elementary school. So I knew by experience that this sickness Annie and I had was not your typical virus.

Doctors began to suspect that perhaps we had picked up Giardia in the lake, or perhaps E-coli from something we had eaten. They tested us for West Nile disease and parasites. Neither of us got better, and I ended up again at the Stanford Hospital Emergency Room. Now, there is something just not right about the valet parking attendant at the emergency room knowing your name. Here we were again!

The Stanford infectious disease team met to try to figure out my case, but no one seemed clear on what was happening. Clearly I had some kind of infection, because my white count was 20,000 (normal range is under 11,000), and apparently my platelet count was up near a million (normal range is about 500). They did scans, chest x-rays, and a spinal tap because they were now worried about Meningitis. One concerning chest x-ray looked like there was a mass in my chest. My doctor, who knew me very well, did not tell me right away about the suspected mass, but suggested we do a CT scan immediately.

Thankfully, there was no mass, and after some round of powerful intravenous antibiotics, I slowly began to improve. In the meantime, Annie improved slightly, but then she got worse. She ended up at Lucille Packard Children's Hospital with doctors trying ceaselessly to figure out what was making her so sick. In the end, we both slowly got better, but doctors were never conclusive on what disease we actually had. It was not a happy, breezy summer for the Pierces to say the least.

Ben then got invited to speak to a large gathering of pastors in the Congo. We sensed Jesus calling him to go. As I write this book, he has just returned from 10 days of amazing ministry to these dear people, preaching in 110 degree heat in the jungle right on the Congo river. He did not have a headache the entire trip and was able to preach every day for hours in that heat.

When he boarded the plane to come home, however, Ben started running a fever of 102. Just another bizarre, painful disease hitting our family again: malaria. The good news is that Ben was a missionary in the Congo in his twenties and has had malaria several times before—nothing that unusual for us at this point.

One of my favorite songs during these dark days was written by my friend, Sara Groves. I would find myself singing these words, driving around in the minivan:

When I get to heaven, I'm gonna go find Job, gonna ask a few hard questions, I want to know what He knows, about what it is he wanted, and what he got instead. About how to be broken, yet faithful.
"What I Thought I Wanted," The Other Side of Something

One family friend, a non-Christian, put it this way,

"Wow, Christy. It seems like forces of darkness are trying to take out your family. God must have some real plans left for you on this earth, because all of you are still here." For my money, she was right on. It was getting kind of funny, really, if you could look at the big picture. The Enemy is stupid, and sometimes he just goes too far. Now, even non-believers were commenting that God must have a purpose for our family to be hit with so many random accidents and diseases.

His plan to foil our efforts only enlightened others to his festering plans. Our story is an opportunity to share with believers as well as friends who are not sure they believe in Jesus that God is bigger than any trial we may face. He really is able to take all the bad stuff and work it together for good. It does not mean you will not face suffering in this life, but with Jesus right beside you, you do not have to go through it alone.

One month before the car on Edgewood Road hit Ben on his bike, I was speaking at the Life in the Spirit conference in Honolulu, Hawaii. At the end of the conference, a lady came to me and said,

"I think I have a word for you, Christy." I smiled politely, but to be real with you, after three days of this conference, I was ready to be by the ocean sipping an umbrella drink with my friends. But I said,

"Sure thing. What do you think God might be saying?" She then said, "The word I hear over your head is 'car crash' and 'cancer.'" The smile on my face froze, and I tried to say something pastoral, along the lines of, "Thanks for sharing, but if God wants me to know that, I think He will show me." Then, I ran over to the two leaders at the conference and said,

"Yikes! Dust me off from that word!"

So, what in the heck do we say about that "word"? Was it the Enemy? Was it God? After two years suffering through a car crash, potential cancer scare (a mass in Ben's brain that turned out to be benign), and another cancer scare with the phantom mass in my chest, here is what I think: The Enemy had a plan to take out our family, and God let me see it ahead of time so we would be better prepared.

I would know it was not just random life events, but actual demonic attacks we needed to fight against. You see, I am a fighter at heart. Nothing makes me more upset than when the Enemy attacks God's people. Yes, we may be hit from time to time with demonic attacks, because we are at war on this earth until we get to heaven, but our God is bigger. We have power to stand and to fight, and when we experience God's deliverance in times like this, our faith only gets stronger.

As we cried out to God in our suffering, the Lord came, and He began to pour His healing and strength into our weak places. We held onto the words of James, who encouraged God's people when he said, "My brothers and sisters, whenever you face trials of any kind, consider it nothing but joy, because you know that the testing of your faith produces endurance; and let endurance have its full effect, so that you may become mature and complete, lacking in nothing (James 1:2-4, NRSV).

One day, I was venting my "Why us, God?" questions about the ongoing illnesses my family was facing. I have found that God does not tend to answer "why" questions often in life. Sometimes, we understand when we look back. Instead of specific answers to my "why" questions, I have found God's answer more often like a loving Father, who cannot fully explain to his kids why they are hurting because they are too young to understand. So, instead He lovingly tells them to trust Him, despite not knowing exactly why. That is just plain hard.

The Apostle Paul put it this way, "….there was given me, a thorn in my flesh, a messenger of Satan, to torment me. Three times I pleaded with God to take it away, but He said to me, 'My grace is sufficient for you, for my power is made perfect in weakness'" (2 Corinthians 12:7-9). For hundreds of years, scholars have disagreed about just exactly what Paul's thorn was, with various guesses: Was it blindness? A demon? Sexual temptation? Illness?

The truth is that no one knows for sure, and I think God left it that way on purpose. The Lord knew His children would face suffering of many different kinds, and that when we do come face-to-face with trials, we need to know that God's grace is sufficient. If we press into Him, His power will pour into us, transforming our weakness into strength.

The Archbishop of Rwanda, E.M. Kolini, is a dear friend of ours. Ben worked with him for three years in Zaire, before it became the Congo. Kolini is one of the most heroic leaders I know when it comes to suffering. He experienced first-hand the forces of evil as the genocide swept over his country and millions of his people died. Kolini and his wife, Freda, lost friends and family members in this horrible tragedy.

Respected by both Hutus and Tutsis alike, the government of Rwanda invited Kolini to leave his home in the Congo to work for reconciliation in Rwanda. Not long after the genocide, Kolini visited us and preached at our church in San Mateo, California. The congregation knew of the stories of genocide and was at a loss as to how to comfort a man who had seen such unbearable suffering in life. What would they say to someone who had family members who were slaughtered? How would this man even be able to preach with such grief and sorrow in his heart?

When Kolini entered the sanctuary, it was reverently silent. When he stepped up to the pulpit to deliver the sermon, he looked out at the congregation, with a smile of joy and peace on his face. His words boomed in the quiet sanctuary,

"Greetings brothers and sisters! Today I bring you greetings, dear friends, from your brothers and sisters in Africa." His words of joy and exhortation seemed so out of place. "They want you to know," he continued, "that they are in Africa, praying for you right now, because of the *trials of abundance* you are facing. For although we suffer, it is a suffering that brings us closer to God."

I wish you could have been there to see the stunned looks of the congregation as Kolini reflected God's authentic joy in the face of suffering. It is a moment I will never forget: A true authority in joy apart from circumstances, his message rattled our faiths.

There is no place God wants to whisper more into our lives than when we are suffering. It is what C.S. Lewis meant when He says that in our pain, God speaks through a megaphone. And yet, during our darkest times, we experience Him as silent, even when He may be shouting at us. We can feel abandoned by the very God who is supposed to be comforting us.

You have a unique life story, which I am sure includes some painful chapters.

I do not know your story, but you can be sure that God has seen it all. In fact, you might be in a fire of suffering right now as you are reading this book. Or, the memory of a time when pain was so intense that you wondered if God had abandoned you entirely might be sweeping over you now.

Please know that I will not be one of those people who pretend to fully know your pain or to understand exactly what it was like to walk in your shoes. I hate it when people do that, especially when I am reeling in pain—only made worse by their quick-fix, "It's all going to be OK" responses.

What I hope to do is to encourage you that God is really, really there with you, and if you cry out to Him, He will not leave you hanging. Whether your pain is healed right away or your suffering is never relieved, I know this for sure: God has not abandoned you, and He wants to whisper to you when you are hurting. I want to spend the rest of this chapter sharing some ways we can experience God in our suffering and hear His quiet whispers in our pain.

God's voice in the darkness

How can we hear God's voice and see Him moving in the chaotic darkness? Before you read these practical ways to hear God's whispers in your darkness, I invite you to take a minute, close your eyes, and ask God to show you which of these practical tools might best help you hear His voice in your suffering.

1 · Be real with your pain before God

Cry out to God with your pain. Ask Him to meet you in the suffering. When we are in great pain, many different feelings threaten to overwhelm us. We can be angry, sad, or disappointed with God, or furious at someone, lonely, or physically hurting. One of the worst things to do at times like this is to try to swallow those huge emotions and bear it all silently. It is not good for our bodies, minds, or spirits to handle pain this way.

In fact, it is not even biblical. The Bible says, "A cheerful heart is good medicine, but a crushed spirit dries up the bones" (Proverbs 17:22). I am not sure how you want to vent your pain to God, but find the way that works for you. Maybe you need to take a walk with Jesus and pour out your heart to Him. Perhaps writing it all down in a journal will be the best way for you to unload your pain to God. Do not bottle it all up inside, but let God know exactly how you feel. And do not worry if you are angry at God. He can handle it.

2 · Ask God to speak louder

Give God a chance. Pray and ask God to speak louder to you in your pain right now. Ask Him to turn up the volume, not just to whisper, but to shout! Pray to Jesus and ask Him for a word, vision, picture, Scripture, or another person to bring comfort. Ask God to whisper to you: *Lord, give me a vision, picture, word, or sign that you see my pain and you are with me.*

3 · Do not be a Lone Ranger when you are suffering

When we are in pain, we tend to isolate ourselves. It is hard enough just to function, much less be with people or talk about our feelings, in the midst of trauma. I have found this especially true with men. I cannot say this strongly enough: It is critical that you find safe people to support you when you are suffering. Whatever it takes, whatever it costs, find these people.

Do not isolate yourself. One of the key ways God is going to whisper to you in your pain is through other people. Find a good counselor, prayer team, healing ministry, pastor, or safe friend. Better yet, try to find all of them! You deserve all the support you can get when you are going through a hard time like this. Do not go it alone because God has historically used people to bring His messages of healing, comfort, and love to His children.

4 · Remember that God does not waste pain

God will use your pain for good, if you will let him. Romans 8:28 ("And we know that God works all things together for good for those who love Him") is not just a bunch of empty words. One of the good things about suffering is God really and truly uses our suffering as that which strengthens our faith. We are transformed in our suffering into stronger, more faithful people. Not only that, but when we have gotten our own Ph.D. in suffering, we are far better equipped to minister to those with similar life struggles. The Bible puts it this way,

> *Praise be to the God and Father of our Lord Jesus Christ, the Father of compassion and the God of all comfort, who comforts us in all our*

troubles, so that we can comfort those in any trouble with the comfort we ourselves have received from God. (2 Corinthians 1:3-4)

One of the people on my prayer teams, Kim, travels with me to minister to others. Kim's husband died when her daughter was only nine and her son was just seven. When we speak on healing, I always want Kim there. God uses her powerfully to pray for healing and comfort those in pain. Kim practically does not need to say a word. Her mercy and compassion are tangible as someone who has been there. We call this "standing in the valley" with those in suffering. When you have been there in that valley, God will use you to minister to others in great power. He will not waste your pain. He will use it to transform you and others if you let Him.

5 · "Trust in the dark what you know to be true in the light"

Bob Munger was an amazing man who mentored many Christian leaders and was a key figure in my husband's life. He had this saying about trusting God in pain:

"Trust in the dark what you know to be true in the light." It was simple, yet profound. You and I have a choice to make when we are in pain. We can choose to intellectually claim the biblical truth that God is with us, even when we do not feel it. You may not know that I am someone with a life-long struggle with low-grade depression. I remember one time specifically I was in an especially dark season, and I was trying to pray, but feeling nothing. It was a foggy day in the Bay Area, and I sensed God lead me outside. I looked up at the fog and the Spirit of the Lord spoke to me saying, *Christy, do you see the sun?* I scoffed. *Actually, no, Lord.* He kept speaking: *Even though you only see the fog, you know the sun is still there, right?* The answer was yes, of course. *That's how it is when you are in this depression. You can't feel me right now, but you know that I'm there.*

At times like this, I often just read the Psalms. Maybe that is because the Psalmists were people who walked by faith despite their own plummets into anger, suffering, and sadness. They knew how to pour out their pain to God, and still claim that God loved them and was with them, even when they could not feel His nearness.

GOD, PLEASE WHISPER TO ME NOW...

Can you remember a painful chapter in your own life, either now or in the past? Did you experience God's whisper during that time of pain? If so, how?

Have you ever experienced God as "silent" when you are hurting?

When you are in pain, do you tend to reach out to others or to isolate?

Give any painful things in your life to God right now. Ask Him to whisper to you, and trust that He knows how to break through any dark clouds in your life, so that you might experience His presence with you.

PRAYER

Lord Jesus, thank you that you are close to the brokenhearted. Thank you that you promise to meet us in pain and that you do not waste my pain. Lord, I give you all my suffering, and I ask you to show up and speak to me. Help me to see where you are and what you are doing in this pain. Please, Jesus, do not just whisper, but in some way that gets through to me, shout louder, so that I can experience your very near, comforting Presence in my suffering. In Jesus' name, Amen.

Rainbows: God Knows Your Unique Colors

All around Him was a halo, like a glowing rainbow shining in the clouds on a rainy day. This is what the glory of God looked like to me, and when I saw it, I fell face down on the ground.
Ezekiel 1:28 (NLT)

For we are God's masterpiece. He created us anew, so that we can do the good things he planned for us long ago.
Ephesians 2:10 (NLT)

Ben could see I was at a point of extreme exhaustion, and a generous friend made it possible for me to go rest in Kauai. My body was weary from two years taking care of family members with brain injuries and fighting the mysterious infectious disease that hit Annie and me. I did not realize how tired I was until I got off the plane in Hawaii, and then slept 16 hours that first night.

That next morning, I went to breakfast and invited Jesus to come join me. I did not really expect to hear anything from God. I was too tired. Still I put worship music on my phone, and I asked God to meet me. The Lord is so gracious when He knows we are so fragile and weak. As I sat looking at the ocean, with the mountains of Kauai in the background, Jesus met me powerfully. I will attempt to describe exactly what happened, though words are hard to find.

I was sitting in a restaurant with my headphones on listening to worship music with my eyes closed. All of a sudden, I saw a very faint picture of Jesus walking toward me. He was smiling, and then as He came closer, He picked me up. He walked, with me in his arms, outside where He lifted me high up into the clouds above the ocean.

Then, I heard His voice say, *Christy, I made this ocean and everything in it. I made these mountains. And I made you. I made you beautiful.* At that point, I began to weep. (It was a little embarrassing because people were nearby, but I did not care. I was so caught up in wonder of God actually speaking to me.) God knew my every thought. He knew how old, worn out, and ugly I felt—a million miles away from feeling beautiful! Then, Jesus said something to me that I hope I will hold in my heart for a very long time: *When are you going to believe that you belong to me? You are mine!*

Somehow, that word touched me more than anything else. I had never felt so completely safe, so secure in the hands of Jesus, so certain that I belonged to the Creator, who saw me as His beautiful daughter. It was overwhelming, and a supernatural peace flooded my weary body. Again, I heard Jesus whisper, *Open your eyes.* When I opened my eyes, there was a huge rainbow over the mountains, with brilliant colors radiating over the waterfalls. Perhaps it was a glimpse of what heaven will look like someday? I had never seen something so beautiful in nature.

At that moment, I sensed the Spirit of God teaching me something very profound about the different ways He speaks to us. Just like the myriad of colors that shine from rainbows, so are the beautifully unique ways God speaks to His children. In this chapter, I am going to try to paint a picture of those many ways God speaks. As you read, I want to encourage you by saying this: **God made you beautiful, and you belong to Him.**

Whether or not you feel it right now, it is true. God knows your heart language, and He knows how to speak to you in unique ways that only you can hear. The colors of your rainbow will be different from other people's way of hearing God, but it is no less powerful or special. As you read some of the unique ways God speaks below, I also have sensed God whispering that He wants to paint new colors on the hearts of those of you who will let Him. What that means is that while you likely experience and hear God in ways that make sense to your heart language, God likely has new ways of hearing His voice for you. If you will give Him freedom to speak to you in fresh ways, God will do that. But it is up to you.

How in the world can I say that? What if one of you reading this asks God to speak to you in new ways and nothing happens? What if you take the courageous step of praying, *Yes, God, I am open to hearing your voice in new ways*—and God is silent? As a pastor, I am aware of the danger of encouraging people that they can hear God for themselves. It is a risky challenge to put out there, if only because of the question: what if a person just does not experience God whispering? What if they get discouraged in their prayer life with God because of what I had said? And yet, I am not backing down. God has called me to encourage you that He is talking to you all the time, and that you can hear His voice more personally.

Therefore, I unashamedly, boldly, passionately urge you to ask God to whisper to you! I am not saying this because I know exactly how God will speak to you. I am not encouraging you to pray this way just because I have faith it will happen. I simply know that Jesus' heart of love for you is way bigger than you can ever imagine. He loves you with an everlasting love, and there is no way He is going to dismiss your prayer of wanting to hear His voice more. There is no way that He is going to let you down when you are trying to hear Him whisper more. It may take some time. It may take some practice. It may take perseverance. But if you seek God, His promise is that He will answer you.

Imagine this with me for a moment. Say one of my kids came to me and said, "Mom, I long to talk to you more, and I really want to hear the things on your heart for me." Would I just silently walk away? No way! I would be overjoyed! I would be thrilled that my child longed to just sit with me, talk with me about the things that mattered to them, and that they wanted to hear my wisdom in return. In the Bible, we are told, "If you then, who are evil, know how to give good gifts to your children, how much more will your Father in Heaven give the Holy Spirit to those who ask Him?" (Luke 11:13).

Unlike others who let you down in life, the Lord will not disappoint you. You may need to be like the persistent widow who asked and asked again. But one thing I know for sure: Faith in God like this will not end in disappointment.

In my whispering journey with God, I have seen some common ways that God speaks to His people, each a different color of the rainbow. For those of you in the more intellectual circles, you might be more familiar with God speaking through preaching or Bible study. For those of you in more charismatic circles, you may be more familiar with God speaking through spiritual gifts like prophecy or words of knowledge.

We are all God's family, though, and we can learn a lot from one another when it comes to hearing God. As I describe below the biblical ways Jesus speaks to His people, I am also going to use modern-day examples and stories of individuals I know personally who have heard God whisper in that way. As you read, I would invite you to notice the ways you most often experience God whisper. I would also invite you to be open to new ways God might be wanting to speak to you. If you find your heart excited and wishing God would speak to you in a new way listed below, pay attention! Some of these new ways of hearing God might just have your name on them.

The rainbow of hearing God's voice: What color are you?

1 · The Bible

One of the primary ways God speaks is through His written Word, the Bible. Reading and studying your Bible is one of the most important ways God will speak to you. Not only that, but as people who want to hear God's voice, we must know our Bible well, or we run the risk of hearing messages that are not God. We must be familiar with God's written word, which will provide us with discernment.   Having said that, I would encourage you to find a translation of the Bible that most helps you hear God's voice. As a master of divinity, I have studied almost every translation of the Bible, including the Hebrew Scriptures and the Greek New Testament. I can say with confidence, then, that there is not one "right" Bible translation that everyone should read. My teenagers, for example, prefer The Message, which is a translation that written in contemporary English. My seminary required we use the New International Version. Regardless, read your Bible! Ask God to speak to you as you read, and He will do that.

2 · Corporate worship and preaching/teaching

The Bible encourages us to "not give up meeting together as some are in the habit of doing" (Hebrews 10:25). We live in a culture of technology spirituality, where you can watch preachers on television, on your computer, and a variety of other sources from your own home—alone. That is great at times, however, there is something powerful and God-breathed about gathering together with other believers for a time of corporate worship and hearing God's word preached. This can be a large church, small church, or home church. It does not matter, but it is important to gather together with other believers. God promises to be there when "two or three are gathered together in his name" (Matthew 18:20). Do we not want to heed His words and dive into the depths of community where we can hear and experience Him as the Body of Christ?

3 · Christian community

This is slightly different from the corporate worship service mentioned above. Christian community is being in relationship with other Christians who will speak truth into your life. If we are disconnected to other people, if we only attend a single church service throughout the week, if we are not willing to be vulnerable with other Christian people, we will only grow so far in hearing God's voice. It is imperative that we find a small group of believers with whom we are really vulnerable if we want to hear God speak into our lives. For me, I can honestly say I would never have learned to hear God whisper without these small groups of believers who helped me grow in hearing God's voice. If you do not have one of these groups, find one! Whatever it takes, whatever it costs, ask God to lead you to an authentic group of believers where you can be fully yourself and fully known.

4 · Nature

Some of us tend to hear God through nature. My husband, Ben, is certainly one of those people. One time, Ben was so discouraged in ministry, he was ready to resign his pastoral position and give up. He was venting to God his anger, disappointment, and plans to throw in the towel, when God led him to pick up a book in his office.

The book was called *Come Away My Beloved* by Francis J. Roberts. It is a book about hearing God through the Holy Spirit. Ben started to read it, but was distracted, because there was a tapping at his office window. Whatever it was kept tapping and tapping and tapping. Frustrated, Ben stopped reading, and went to the window. At the window was a dove, resting on the window sill.

(Ben did not get the miraculousness of this situation quite yet.)

He tried shooing it away, but it looked him in the dead in the eye, unhindered, and kept tapping. Finally, Ben had a "duh" revelation from God (as we like to say): God was right there, in front of him, speaking through nature. Ben was reading a book about the Holy Spirit, and there was a real live dove starring him in the face. At that moment, Ben made the connection (a dove is used in the Bible to refer to the Holy Spirit). Talk about God speaking!

God spoke to Ben in that moment, and Ben felt like God saw him. That was a turning point of understanding that God was speaking directly to him in a way that got through. Many of us experience God better in nature. When Ben wants to hear God, he will drive to a special place at the ocean he likes. I will go to Filoli Gardens, a botanical garden near our house. My friend, Cindy, experiences Jesus most when she is walking through the woods on a sunny day with her horse. Some people will go for a hike and invite Jesus to come along and speak. If God speaks to you through nature, lean into that. Spend more time in God's creation if it tends to be an "open window into heaven" kind of spot for you.

5 · Other people

Have you ever had a friend call at just the right time when you needed a word of encouragement? Ever go to see a counselor or pastor, and it was as if God spoke His very words to you through them? So many times, we need others to have faith for us, when our faith is tired. I cannot begin to count the times when I have been discouraged and weary in my life and a good friend will e-mail or text at the very minute I needed to hear that encouragement. We need each other. We need to be open to God speaking into our lives through others, and we need to be people who listen to God and reach out to others when He nudges us to do that. Following God is not a "Lone Ranger" kind of journey. Speaking of other people, some of the most important people who can be the voice of God speaking are not even adults, but children.

6 · God speaks to us through our children

Jesus said it best when he said, "Let the little children come to me, and do not hinder them, for the Kingdom of heaven belongs to such as these" (Matthew 19:14). I could write a whole book about how God speaks to us through our children. Countless times, God has spoken to me through my kids, and I am sure I have only recognized some of those messages.

A few months ago, Corey and I were leaving Target, and she looked at me and said something that still gives me chicken skin (a funny term for "the chills" that Hawaiians use). Corey said to me in her quiet, wise, 12-year-old voice, "Mom, I think God may have whispered something to me to tell you, but I'm not sure?" She stopped and I studied her sweet face, so innocent and trusting. "I believe that God told me the reason our family has gone through all these painful years is that we are some sort of vanguard in the spiritual war. These hard times somehow are making us into stronger people to lead some sort of battle." Sipping my Target Diet Coke, I looked at Corey, and burst into tears. If anyone else had told me that, I would likely have smiled and dismissed it with a "Thanks for sharing" and forgot all about it! Coming from Corey, who has suffered so much, with such a humble heart, was like water pouring into my weary soul.

Annie is my little prophet. She hears God all the time. She has dreams and visions that seem like they can only be from God. I had two friend who were trying to make a big job decision, and they were describing it to me with five-year-old Annie listening. After they were done talking, Annie looked straight at them and said calmly,

"I think God is telling me that you should take this job because if you do, it won't be like the last job that was a big mistake." Annie literally had no way of knowing that the last job was a long, painful chapter in their lives. When she ran off to jump on the trampoline, they looked at me with stunned expressions and asked,

"What was that?! Is she 25 years old?"

Just last week, Benji and his friend were in the back seat of my minivan. Benji's friend, Zach, was saying demons were not real spirits. Benji said plainly, "Demons are real, Zach, don't you believe the Bible?" Zach responded by saying that, yes he believed the Bible, but that he thought demons were only around when Jesus lived. Benji responded, "Not true. Demons are real today. But Zach, the cool thing is that Jesus has given us power to send them away. Isn't that way cool?" Zach said,

"Maybe fear is some kind of demon?" I had been listening quietly, but then piped up to encourage Zach,

"Yes, Zach, fear can definitely be a demon. You can send it away in Jesus' name." Benji then, as children do, spoke something that seemed so wise for his age,

"Zach, I think the worst kind of demon is called 'no self-confidence.'" Wow. I stopped and turned around. In that moment, I knew that was God speaking. That demon, "no self-confidence," as Benji said, had been tearing us all down: Ben, Benji, me. Benji's word exposed the lie of the Enemy, and our family prayed that night, commanding it to go in Jesus' name. Was that God? I think so.

Benji has also been asking the painfully honest question of when we were going to open New Hope again. It has been heartbreaking because we have all missed our church since having to take medical leave. The church has closed down. The congregation moved on. But Benji will not stop. He keeps saying it, touching on the wound of sadness and disappointment. But as a family, we agree the word for that question is this: New Hope Peninsula Church was chapter one. Chapter two is a bigger mission: New Hope Peninsula Ministries. Benji had been speaking God's answer all along; we just did not recognize it.

Do you have kids? If not, do you know children that love God? Listen to them! God has a special way of speaking through them that will truly minister to you.

7 · Circumstances

Circumstances may seem like the plainest way of God speaking, but He certainly orchestrates the events of our life to speak to His will. A single woman came to my office once when I was a pastor to single adults. She told me that she wanted to hear from God about whether she was supposed to go to Fuller Seminary, and she was angry with God because He had been silent so far.

So, I started asking questions: Have you asked other people if they feel seminary is a good fit for your gifts? Have you gone down to Fuller to meet with the professors and admissions folks there, to see if it feels like a place you are called to go? Her answer was "no" on both counts. Have you applied to Fuller and looked at what is required financially and how many years it will take? No again. You see, all of these are circumstances through which God may have confirmed whether her call to seminary was His call or not.

I told her the story about God and the parked car: Sometimes God is calling us to step out of fear, or being paralyzed, just to get our car moving. It is easier for God to steer a car that is moving, than one that is just parked. Often, we wait for God to send a lightening bolt from the sky to show us the entire path, but He has continually chosen to show us the step-by-step instead. As an aside, here is a good prayer to pray if you are seeking guidance and direction. If you sense God is nudging you in a certain direction, you can simply ask God, *Lord, it seems like this is the way you want me to go. I am going to keep heading this direction, but give you complete permission to close the door if it's not something you want for my life.* Keep your eyes open and your ears tuned, for the quiet whispers are often God speaking through circumstances in your life.

8 · Gut feelings

I would be a rich woman if I had a dollar for every time people say they do not hear from God, but that they "just get these gut feelings." Many times, God speaks to us through what we call intuition or a gut feeling. It is no less important than a prophetic revelation. In fact, it is often what the Bible calls a "spiritual gift of wisdom" (1 Corinthians 12:8).

However, we discount it as only a feeling and not of God. How do we know if it is God or if it is just a feeling? We will talk more about that in chapter nine, but know that God often speaks this way. Just know that is a matter of discernment and learning to know yourself. It is also important to filter feelings through the Bible. (The woman, for example, who told me she had a "gut feeling" that God was telling her she should have sex with her boyfriend was not lining up her feelings with what Scripture teaches. Her "gut feeling" was, in fact, directly contradictory to what the Bible says.) Pay attention to your gut feelings, though. Write them down in a journal, ask God to confirm them if they are His voice, and ask others for discernment.

9 · Journaling

If you do not own a journal, please go buy one. It will be money well spent. Throughout the centuries, people seeking to hear God have written down what they think God might be saying to them. I have practiced journaling for my 20 years of following God, and it has consistently been a pivotal tool that God uses in my prayer life. My husband, Ben, loves to journal and says, "Somehow when I journal, my thoughts disentangle themselves as I write them out on paper." I could not agree more. Often, my daughter and I will take our journals, Bibles, and worship music to Filoli Gardens or another quiet place. When I am alone, I put on my worship music on my iPod, I read my Bible, and then I write a letter to God in my journal. Usually, it is just plain venting to God of where I am at that moment and my calling out to Him for help. It is not professional, perfect, or even faith-filled at times.

My entries look more like, *Dear Jesus, here I am. I'm tired, and lonely and in pain. I thank you that you are always with me. Please just speak!* After I am done writing to God, I have learned to stop and to listen. This is the hard part: waiting. It is hard because I am impatient, have a million other things to do, and want God to speed it up. However, I have learned something invaluable: God is not in a hurry. He wants to hang out with me, hear my heart, speak quietly to me, and meet me right where I am. If you have never done this, please try it. Write letters to God in your journal, but then ask Him to speak. If this is new for you (and you are not alone!), just give it two minutes! Write down anything you hear at all, whether it makes sense or not, and "put it on the shelf." I am pretty sure you will be surprised, if stay with it, the number of times God is speaking to you when you thought it was just a fleeting thought of your own.

You need to keep at this and over time, God will keep speaking to you in ways that get louder and louder. It is a spiritual discipline of making time to be with God, to listen for that still, small voice, and to do what we Westerners are not good at—waiting! We spend a lot of time talking at God but very little time listening.

The first year I was at Fuller Seminary, I had not slowed down much from my Washington, D.C., everything-is-a-frenzy lifestyle. In fact, I was still working for Elizabeth Dole from California doing advance work on the West Coast. I was doing my masters of divinity full time, working for the government, working part- time to earn money, and helping a professor as a teaching assistant. I rarely slept and I never stopped to hear God.

One day, at Fuller Seminary's prayer garden, I took a minute between classes to stop and try to hear God. And, as He graciously does, He was there ready to answer me: *Christy, I want you to stop all the frenzy. Every Friday, I want you to just seek my face.* What a relief! I had a permission slip from God to stop the chaos and just be quiet, meditate, and be with God. Boy, was I excited! Friday, I got all prepared, and I took my Bible, my journal, my worship tapes, and headed up the mountain to a monastery. I got there and searched for a quiet spot in the garden. I found a bench. But that bench was too hard, so I searched for another. That spot was too breezy, so I kept searching. Finally, I found a place to pray, and I set out my Bible, journal, worship music, and started to pray and seek God. I only lasted 45 minutes. I just could not take all that stillness. It was too quiet. There were no people around, and I could not focus on just hearing God.

So, I packed up my stuff, and went to Ross Dress For Less to shop. The next week I went back. This time, I stayed for an hour. The next week, I was there for two hours, then the following week, for half a day. Pretty soon, I could not wait until Friday so I could head up the mountain and just be with Jesus for the whole day. My point is this: Give yourself a break. If you do not consider yourself the hearing-God-contemplative type, think again. Possibly you have never given yourself permission to just begin where you are—even if that is at the very beginning—and keep persevering, until you cannot wait to just hang out with God in a quiet place. You might just surprise yourself. (A word to the wise: Leave the cell phone at home. E-mail and Instagram are just too enticing when you first start out practicing this!)

10 · Worship music

What kind of music moves you? Just as hearing God can be different for everyone, so is the kind of music that moves us to really worship God. Some of us like hymns, others like contemporary worship music, some of us like rap, or pop, or whatever. Whatever worship music draws you closer to God, use it in your prayer life.

For me, this is perhaps one of the most important tools in my tool bag when I am trying to hear God's voice. Worship music brings me in touch with God like no other tool. Unfortunately, we pastors have done a poor job, I believe, when it comes to helping people understand how to worship with music.

So many of my friends who are new to the church will ask to cut out all the music and get right to the sermon. However, what I think they actually mean most of the time is that they do not get the purpose of the music. They look around and see other people in church who are moved by the worship, who know the words and who may even be lifting their hands. Those new in church may just be too uncomfortable not knowing the words or not knowing the purpose of worship itself to really engage in the worship. We need to disciple others when it comes to the value of worship music. We need to give them permission to find their own worship style that brings them close to God. It is such an awesome way God has spoken to His people throughout all of human history.

11 · Hearing God's voice and the Holy Spirit

In the Scriptures, we are told about gifts of the Spirit, and this is incredibly important to understand if we want to hear the whispering voice of God. Let me be frank: I am saddened that too many of God's people have limited the way God speaks to just those ways they have already experienced in life. I believe it makes God sad, because there are so many ways in which He wants to bless His children and to speak to them, if they will just be willing to learn new things.

I have said it before, but it is true: The Holy Spirit has gotten a bad rap. If we want to hear God, it is a good thing to understand that Jesus communicates to us in a myriad of ways through the Holy Spirit, which is not limited to Bible study and preaching, though these are very important. Still, there are numerous other spiritual gifts listed in the Bible, which many Christians have never experienced personally, so they have put aside as moot.

Decades ago, I was on staff in a church that did not believe in the gifts of the Holy Spirit. The staff believed that I had a prophetic gift, and they trusted me, but mostly they were skeptical when it came to people experiencing God through what they called the "charismatic gifts." At a staff meeting one day, a big discussion erupted, and it got pretty heated. We were doing a series on the Holy Spirit, and the preaching pastor said,

"You guys, I'm preaching on the Holy Spirit, and I'm thinking I'll leave out the gifts like prophecy, word of knowledge, tongues, healing and dreams." He literally said that he was "worried that people might get the wrong idea and think we are one of those weird, charismatic kind of churches." A few pastors laughed, but the majority of the room was silent.

Then, a fascinating thing happened. One by one, half of the room of pastors began raising their hands and "admitting" that they were actually sort of charismatic themselves, because they had the gift of prophecy, healing, tongues, or words of knowledge. There were undercover charismatics right beneath our very noses!

I am hoping that I have not offended some of you reading, and if I have not yet, bear with me, because by the end of the book I might be able to offend the rest of you. This is a universally-touchy subject, but I am diving into the deep end nonetheless. It is unfortunate that just the word "charismatic" has gotten a bad connotation. In the Bible, that word in the original Greek language simply means "gift." In the Bible, all the gifts are from God.

Regardless of our theology, I think it is dangerous to block out half of the spiritual gifts listed in the Bible, as some pastors do. Not only that, I think it is even more prideful to say, "We don't want to become one of those churches." Many of these churches on the mission field now, by the way, are moving in spiritual power regularly and are exploding because of it. Gifts like prophecy, healing, words of knowledge, and miracles are part of the norm in their weekly worship services, regardless of their denominational affiliation.

I know, I know: I said you can hear God without being weird, right? Well, here is what I meant. You can destroy the negative pictures you may have in your mind of what it looks like to be a person who hears God speak to them, and you can instead allow God's voice in draw you in new ways into a deeper friendship with Jesus. Unintentionally, some of us have become Christians strong in the Word, but weak in the things of the Spirit. If I throw my five-year-old daughter a birthday party and give her many gifts I know will bless her, will I only let her open half of the gifts? Of course not! I adore her, and I want her to have all the gifts that will bring her joy. That may seem like a silly example, but I think you catch my drift. God knows how hard this life will be, and all the suffering we will encounter. That is exactly why God graciously gives all the gifts to His church, so that we will be fully equipped to "fight the good fight" and reach as many people as possible. My friend, Stefanie, has many great prophetic gifts and visions from God. My family would not have made it through these past two years of pain without her constant encouragement and prayers. Stefanie often says,

"Life is hard enough without the prophetic. I don't know how people make it without prophetic revelations, dreams and visions from God." That may be her view, but I tend to agree. In this next section, then, I am going to describe some of those spiritual gifts that are not as familiar for some Christians. Following each gift will be a biblical explanation as well as modern-day examples of "normal people" operating in these gifts.

Dreams

DEFINITION A dream is a message given by the Lord to a person as they sleep. These dreams are typically symbolic in nature, although on occasion they can be a literal description of things to come.

BIBLICAL REFERENCES Daniel, Joseph, Philip

MODERN-DAY EXAMPLE Chapter 10 is loaded with examples of how God speaks through dreams, and how to interpret them. It is important to understand your dreams and know which ones are from God, which are from the Enemy, or which are your own unconscious feelings.

Prophecy and prophetic words

DEFINITION Prophecy is when we get a sense, a phrase, or an impression from God that carries with it an aspect of foreshadowing.

BIBLICAL REFERENCES In the Old Testament, prophets such as Isaiah, Jeremiah, Micah, and others declared God's plans and promises in a way that looked toward the future. Because they were in the biblical role of prophet, they had 100 percent accuracy because they were the chosen mouthpieces of the Lord before Jesus came. In the New Testament, we see the gift of prophecy being poured out on believers through the Holy Spirit. The gift of prophecy is listed as a spiritual gift in Romans 12:6 and in 1 Corinthians 12, 13, and 14.

MODERN-DAY EXAMPLE My friend, Jordan Seng, is a worldwide speaker on the prophetic and hearing God's voice. He says this about prophecy: "God has this way of telling you things ahead of time, so that when it happens, it still surprises you—even though He told you ahead of time." I love that description of prophecy, and it is one of the simplest I have heard that makes sense.

Jordan operates in the gift of prophecy often. I highly recommend his book, *Miracle Work*, which gives many good examples of the gift of prophecy operating today through believers.

MODERN-DAY EXAMPLE Ben and I travelled to India with Jack and Myrna Klassen to plant churches among the untouchables. On our first trip to India, our prayer leader, Sharon, heard God speak a prophetic word to her about their future trip, specifically that this trip will be their first trip of many back to India. They laughed at the time. As I write this book, they have been back to India 13 times in the past 15 years! God has used them powerfully to minister to the untouchable people in India.

Visions and pictures

DEFINITION A vision is a visual picture (sometimes very faint), which comes from God to the mind of a believer and is a revelation from God about something past, present, or future.

BIBLICAL REFERENCES The Apostle Paul, Jeremiah, Isaiah, Joseph, the Apostle John in the book of Revelation

MODERN-DAY EXAMPLE When I get pictures or visions, it is not at all like the Apostle Paul's big experiences of knowing a friend caught up in the third heaven as in 2 Corinthians 12:2 or anything like that. It is more like a faint impression or picture, almost like watching a fuzzy picture on the television. I have learned to focus on the picture with my eyes closed, and it will often become clearer. How do I know it is from God? The only way to find out is to do what the Bible says, to "test the spirits" (1 John 4:1) and to get discernment. When I share these visions, they are confirmed to be from Him because often they represent something I could not have known apart from His supernatural leading.

Words of knowledge

DEFINITION: A word of knowledge is a specific word that God reveals to a believer that he or she would have no way of knowing without God's direct revelation.

BIBLICAL REFERENCE: The gift called "word of knowledge" is mentioned in 1 Corinthians 12:8.

MODERN-DAY EXAMPLE: Years ago in Kansas City, I joined a group of people who were trying to learn to hear God's voice. We were all rookies to the core. Humble and armed with nothing but a Bible and a willingness to learn, we would read Scriptures about people who heard God. We hosted a human laboratory and invited someone from the group to be the "guinea pig," to sit in the middle of the group, to let us practice hearing God in prayer. We did not know each other very well, and one night, a quiet woman raised her hand and got into the "guinea pig" chair. We surrounded her and asked how would she like us to pray. She was silent and eventually said she would rather not say, but wanted to see if God showed us anything. Well, that was strange, especially since none of us knew what the heck we were doing. But, this was a safe place to try. So we did. For ten minutes, we were all silent, until one other lady in the group said,

"OK, this is really weird, and I'm sure this isn't a word from God, but all I hear in my mind is the word 'cat.' Does that mean anything to you?" The next thing we knew, the woman burst into tears and began to sob uncontrollably. After several minutes of us staring at her in surprise, she looked up, with tears running down her face, and said,

"My cat just died, and he was my only friend." I have never forgotten that word of knowledge, because it is a look into God's heart for people. No one in that room could ever have known that the word "cat" could mean anything to her. But God did. That word of knowledge showed this sad woman that God saw her pain. The courage of that group to pray, and the courage of that woman to risk being our experimental test-run collided in a beautiful moment where God broke through and blessed everyone at once through what the Bible calls a word of knowledge. My strong belief is that the very best way you can learn to hear God's voice is by doing stuff like this in real-life testing grounds, a safe small group of people who are reading a book like this, with the Bible, and being willing to pray for one another.

Word of wisdom/discernment

DEFINITION: An insight into a situation or person's life that carries extraordinary wisdom because it is a direct revelation from God about the person and his or her situation.

BIBLICAL REFERENCE: Acts 27:31-32

MODERN-DAY EXAMPLE: My friends, Pam and Dan Chun, have big ears. Not literally big ears, of course, but in the Spirit, because they hear from God in extraordinary ways through the gift, word of wisdom. When they speak, they often say things that are truly right from God's heart to the people they minister to. They do not always realize it, because they are very humble people, but God uses them powerfully through this gift.

Dan regularly calls me with "a sense" or ideas that are often God-breathed and minister deeply to me. He does not always realize that they are direct messages from God, but I do. Just this past year, God let me be involved in a story that showed this gift in action. A Hawaii pastor asked me to help a single mom with four children who was flown to a Stanford hospital for a heart transplant two days before Christmas. There were no fathers in the picture. A young Stanford student, Tristan, was the oldest child, and who was valiantly trying to hold his siblings together over Christmas hoping their mom would survive. Pam Chun was praying for me as we ministered to this family, and told me, "Christy, I think you're going to play an important role in this family's situation later, but we can't see it right now." The four kids, Tristan, Kiana, Isaiah, and Tryton stayed with us for two weeks over Christmas. The three younger children eventually flew home to Hawaii to live with their pastor, Kainoa and his wife, Danielle. Several days after they left, Tristan texted me to urgently come to the hospital to pray for his mom. Driving to the emergency room, I was not halfway there when Tristan texted me two simple words: "She died." My heart breaking, I ran up to her hospital room to find Tristan, weeping by her bedside, holding her hand. He was singing through his tears,

"Blessed be Your name, on the road marked with suffering. Blessed be Your name…" Tristan is one of the bravest, most Spirit-filled young men I know. It has been a huge honor to know him and his family and to walk alongside them through this valley. Through it all, I have seen Jesus take care of them all, despite the road of suffering. Pam had been right.

GOD, PLEASE WHISPER TO ME NOW...

Has there ever been a time in your life when you think God may have spoken to you? Maybe it was seeing a rainbow? Perhaps it was through someone who called at just the right time? Possibly it was through a dream or picture? Take a minute and write that down here, and share that time with your small group.

Listed in this chapter are many unique ways in which God speaks to people. Which ones tend to be the ones that you have experienced most so far? Which ones seem weird or unusual to you? Are there any new ways of hearing God that touched you in this chapter or that you wish you could experience personally?

Are you open to God speaking to you in some new ways? Why or why not? What is exciting about that to you? What makes you feel anxious about that?

PRAYER

Lord, thank you that you speak in so many different ways, as distinct as the colors of a rainbow. God, I thank you for the many times you have spoken to me, even if I have forgotten them or not realized it at the time. God, I want to hear you more and in new ways. Would you please speak to me in some ways that are fresh and new? I give myself to you, and I open myself to all the colors of the rainbow, and I give you permission to speak to me however you wish. In Jesus' name, Amen.

9

Is That You, God, or Just Spicy Pizza?

And His sheep follow Him because they know His voice.
But they will never follow a stranger; in fact they will
run away from him because they do not recognize a
stranger's voice.
John 10:4-5

Dear friends, do not believe every spirit, but test the
spirits to see whether they are from God.
1 John 4:1

It was a beautiful, warm night in Hawaii, and we were just leaving the Honolulu Convention Center after teaching a session to youth on hearing God's voice. My prayer team and I were ready to kick back, relax, and have a burger somewhere on the beach before we headed back for our final session the next day. Kim was waving for a taxi, and we were just about to jump into the cab when I heard a voice behind me shouting,

"Christy! Wait! I have one more question!" I turned around and saw Julie, one of the teens we had just met, running down the escalators, jumping down two steps at a time. Breathless, she reached us, and then blurted out this funny question, "Christy! How do I know if it's God really speaking or just the spicy piece of pizza I ate last night?" I laughed and said,

"Julie, that is an AWESOME question!"

Middle and high school kids I meet today have a refreshing hunger to hear God for themselves. One high school guy put it this way,

"I want to experience Jesus talking to me for real and not just what my parents or pastor say about how God speaks." Julie articulately summed up the questions many people (regardless of their age) have about hearing God's voice: How do I know if the whispers, pictures, or dreams I have are really from God? I love that Julie was willing to be real with that fear, in such a down-to-earth way. How do we know it is God and not spicy pizza?

More specifically, how can I tell if the words I am hearing are from God, my own voice, the Enemy, or just some wacky thought that crossed my mind? In this chapter, my hope is that you will be encouraged that it is very possible for you to know the difference. In addition, I hope to calm the fears of many who want to hear God more but are afraid of hearing wrong. ("Hearing God wrong" is a common fear, and when we slip into it, we can spiral into the "what if" scenarios that keep us paralyzed from even trying.)

The spirals may go something like this in our head: *What if I'm wrong, and make a mistake? What if I offend someone and look like an idiot? What if this blows up my church? What if God tells me to take a job in India but I really wanted to live in Los Angeles? What if God tells me to buy a bullfrog and name him Jack?* See what I mean? Those "what if" questions can make you crazy, and they can certainly keep you stuck when it comes to practicing hearing God for yourself. I know from experience. I used to go there myself, and I am very familiar with the ugly cycle it takes you down. Having done this stuff for about 20 years, trust me when I tell you I have heard pretty much every question you can imagine. Let me reassure you, if you have some fears when it comes to hearing God's voice, you are not alone! I am hoping this chapter will help answer some of your worries and move you into greater freedom to experience the joy of hearing your Father in heaven speaking to you.

"God, how do I know if this is really you?"

I remember the doctors telling me plainly, without much comfort, "Christy, you have many medical issues that make it pretty much impossible that you will ever have children." They had medical reasons to say that, and I knew they were trying to be realistic, but I still sank into a pretty deep depression. After a lot of research and tons of prayer, Ben and I felt God speaking to us to follow the doctors' advice on infertility treatments. We have been very public about this painful journey, because we have found many other couples are facing similar struggles.

It is a painful journey, and couples must really listen to the Holy Spirit because what is right for one couple might not be right for another. In our case, we felt God said yes to the in vitro fertilization (IVF) path. Again, the Stanford doctors were very cautious that any medical treatment would work for us, and they gave us about a 10 percent chance of actually having kids even with IVF. They were even more discouraged when after all the needles and surgeries, my body only produced three eggs. They bumped down the probability to two percent. The doctor later told me that he did not know of a clinic in the world that would have gone forward with those odds, but for some reason, he did. One of the nurses went to our church, and I pulled her aside one day and asked her,

"We have a group of people praying for our fertility process, and they like to pray specifically. Can you tell us what we should be praying for?" She looked at me and said,

"Pray that all three would become eight cell embryos." So, that was our prayer. I did not really understand that medical jargon, but I asked our prayer team to pray specifically for this to happen. I will never forget the day she called me, practically shouting with joy, "Christy! God answered your prayers! It's a miracle! You are pregnant!" Nine months later, our Corey was born.

It is a funny thing that when you pray and pray for something, you later may forget that it was a miracle. For our precious little baby Corey Belle, a miracle baby, developed colic and screamed like a monkey five hours every night for three months. Like clockwork at five p.m., Corey would enter into the state of high-pitched screeching and beet-red face that did not stop no matter what we did. Oh yes, we tried it all: the drives on the freeway, the car seat on top of the dryer, warm baths, 98 different kinds of milk, and even *Baby Mozart*. You name it. We tried it. But the ear-piercing screams went on for over 90 days. One night, the phone rang, and I grabbed it and practically shouted a hello over Corey's loud crying. It was my Stanford doctor, and he was trying to tell me (as best he could above Corey's screams) that if I ever wanted another baby, I should come in as soon as possible. I was stunned. I held the phone out for him to hear Corey's monkey screech and said,

"Are you CRAZY?! Do you hear this? I can barely make it through the day much less have another baby right now!"

But, I put it before the Lord. God's ways are not always our ways, right? At least that is what the Bible tells us. But honestly, this was such a huge decision that I had to be sure. We were on vacation in Mississippi, and I drove myself out to our family's farm and turned off the car. Sitting alone, staring at the lake, I laid myself bare: *Lord, the doctor said I should do another round of IVF, and you alone know the pain of that—the needles, surgery, money, waiting for the call. Jesus, I need to know, for sure, if you really want me to do it.* Quietly, I sat, and then I heard a quiet whisper, *Yes, Christy, I want you to do it.*

Was this really God? I had to ask Him again (this was too big not to get a confirmation—twice), and I did not want to miss it. So, I started again, *Lord, is this really you? If this is really you, will you confirm it somehow?* Quiet. So, I turned the car key, started the car, and I got ready to drive off. But then I hear God whisper, *Christy, turn to Romans 4:18.* I opened the Bible and it said,

> *Against all hope, Abraham in hope believed and so became the father of many nations, just as it had been said to him, "So shall your offspring be." Without weakening in his faith, he faced the fact that his body was as good as dead—since he was about a hundred years old—and that Sarah's womb was also dead. Yet he did not waver through unbelief regarding the promise of God, but was strengthened in his faith and gave glory to God, being fully persuaded that God had power to do what he had promised.*

In that moment, God poured out on me a deep peace and joy as I read the passage, and I knew it was the Living God speaking to me. Ben and I prayed over this word, and we both sensed that we needed to trust God's promise of another child and move forward with another round of IVF. But that was not all. In addition, I felt God nudge me to not hold back about sharing what happened on that Mississippi farm. So, I did. I told the doctors, my neighbors, and the church staff. I did not shout it from the rooftops or anything, but I sensed strongly God wanted me to be obedient and to tell people what I had heard.

Did people think I was a little crazy? Perhaps that I HAD eaten a spicy piece of pizza and was hearing things? Well, I am pretty sure some of them did, but it did not matter. I knew that I had to share the story each time He nudged me.

Finally, the big day of my surgery came, and they only ended up with one egg to implant. The doctor surprised me by saying,

"Well, all it takes for a miracle is one egg, right?" He had seen Corey's miracle, so we all had hope. Confidently, I waited for the phone call, and when it rang, I picked it up and waited to hear the good news.

"Christy?" the nurse said, "I'm really sorry to tell you this, but you are not pregnant." Shocked and devastated, I called my friend, Sharon, and wept. Sharon wept with me on the phone and cried out to God,

"Lord, you promised! Lord, please show us what's happened and comfort Christy." I sunk into a deeper depression and could barely drag myself onto the airplane two days later, where Ben and I were speaking at a conference in Georgia on faith in God. (Talk about irony!) Those poor people in Georgia got me for their speaker, and thank God, strong Ben was there to stand in the gap for us. They lovingly surrounded us with their prayers and support.

Angry at God

I was in a crisis of faith and was, quite honestly, furious at God. After all, God had told me to tell all those people the assurance of the promise I got in Mississippi, and now I looked like an idiot. I began to question everything. Did I really hear from God at all? Did God really speak to people like this? Did God love me, and was He faithful to His promises? One day, I was venting my anger at God, saying, *Jesus, why did you let this happen? And why did you make me tell all those people?* God seemed silent and distant as I poured out my heart to Him.

Stanford doctors called again, excited about a new medicine from Europe, and they talked us into one more try. Like a robot, I went through all the needles and surgeries, but had no faith at all. Hope seemed to break through the clouds when the doctors told us that we needed to do the surgery on Easter day. Suddenly, our church family, who had been grieving with us, was full of faith. They were even so lighthearted as to joke that we were "going on an egg hunt on Easter day."

That Easter, I went to the hospital for the surgery, with a glimmer of hope, thinking that maybe God would do a miracle, for why would He bring everything down to Easter day and then not come through?

Still groggy after the surgery, I heard cries of joy from the woman in the room next to me, as she heard they got 25 eggs from her surgery. This new technique could really do wonders. Then, my doctor came into to see me, and with deep compassion in his eyes, said to me, "Christy, I don't know how to tell you this, but we didn't get any eggs at all. Zero. I'm so sorry." I looked up at him and these words came out of my mouth before I could even think straight,

"Thank you for all you've done. I believe that God has told me we will have a baby someday, and that might sound crazy to you, but I know I need to stop the medical treatments now and wait." I do not know why I said that, especially since I left the hospital that day with less faith than ever in God whispering. Every day, I tried to keep going, just going through the motions. Those of you who have been depressed know what I mean. You make yourself get up, put your clothes on, and keep going.

One day, I was venting my sadness and anger to God, and through the fog of my despair, I heard God quietly whisper, *Christy, in some way you don't yet understand, I will bring more glory to myself through this "no" than through a "yes."* My response was an angry, *Right God! As if there could be anything that would bring You more glory than showing people you can do a medical miracle of a baby from one egg!* Ben and I continued to go on with life, not any more faith-filled, and then several months later (you guessed it), yep—I am pregnant—the old-fashioned way.

Then, I heard God whisper, *Even though Sarah's womb was dead, they had faith that God had power to do what He had promise*d (Romans 4:19). Nine months later, Annie was born. The doctors said it was a medical miracle. Two years later, our boy, Benji is born, and no one quite knows what to do with *that* little boy miracle. Gram, my mother-in-law, likes to joke,

"Buy two and get one free!" We are very real and honest about this painful infertility story and how God whispers in our pain. In fact, we pray often for those going through infertility struggles and see many people healed who end up with children. Sometimes that happens through the miracle of their own bodies, and other times it is through a beautiful adoption story. Not everyone gets pregnant, and in this journey of pain and confusion, it is normal to be angry or sad. God can meet us in both places. When we pray for those in pain like this, we rarely see a situation in which God does not speak to people in this valley of despair in a way that brings hope and encouragement.

Signs that help us know if it is God and not spicy pizza!

In college, I started out majoring in petroleum engineering, but ended up an economics major. What I do know about me is that I like to analyze things and make sure what I believe is consistent with truth. I have carried that analytical part of me into this ministry of hearing God because I think it is important we have some healthy filters through which to see truth. How can you know that what you are hearing is from God "for true life" (as my daughter Annie says)? How do you know? What can you do to discern the still, small voice you are hearing?

In this section, I want to drill down, and get really practical by discussing some ways you can discern where the voices, words, pictures, and dreams really come from. Not everything we hear is from God, right? But there are some typical signs that might help you recognize a whisper from God in your life. As we have already discussed, not everyone senses God in the same way, and your way of hearing God will be different from someone else. At the same time, there are some telltale signs that, if you pay attention, will help you know if God is really speaking to you.

As the Bible says, "Follow the way of love and eagerly desire spiritual gifts, especially the gift of prophecy" (1 Corinthians 14:1). Prophecy is one spiritual gift that we have already discussed that involves hearing God's voice about future events, but the same principle applies to other ways of hearing God. Over time, you learn to recognize the whispers that are from God and the ones that are not. You will begin to experience some familiar ways that the Spirit of God is trying to get your attention. In those moments, you sense God is saying to you, *Stop. Listen. Pay attention because this is likely God's voice speaking to you.* What do those look like?

Test the Whispers!

Listed below are some typical signs that can help you discern if a whisper is really from the Holy Spirit. Not all of them need to be present to know if it is a whisper from God, but you will see that they provide a good filter to screen what you are hearing.

1 · The message is consistent with the Bible

A key way we test God's words is to make sure they are consistent with the word of God. For example, if you hear, *Go rob a bank,* you can be darn sure that is not from God. This is an extreme example, of course, but you get it. Reading and knowing your Bible is critical when it comes to testing God's whispers, because nothing you hear from the Living God will contradict what is in the Word of God.

2 · It happens during worship

For me, the clearest times I hear God whisper is often during times of worship. This can mean in corporate worship, like in a church service, or it can be in my retreat times with God. It can also be a vision while I am listening to my favorite worship tune. Regardless, God knows this is my heart language, and there is something about being in an atmosphere of worship that creates open windows to heaven for me.

If that is true for you, I would pay attention to the senses, words, or pictures that pop into your mind while you are spending time with God in worship. If that is not you, I would encourage you to try an experiment: Close your eyes during worship, and ask God to speak to you. You might be surprised at what you hear or see. Jot that down in your journal, however faint it may seem, and ask God for confirmation if it is from Him.

3 · Sounds God-y

My husband, Ben (with his notorious "Ben-isms") says, "Well, now that sounds God-y to me!" It is Ben's way of saying that his gut feeling, after walking with God and knowing Him a long time, is that this whisper sounds like something His Father in Heaven would say. Think about it: If your best friend were to send you a letter, and not sign her name, you might well know who it is from because you are familiar with how she sounds. The Bible says, "My sheep follow me because they know my voice" (John 10:27). Hanging out with Jesus over your lifetime will help you grow in knowing His voice.

4 · The whisper is not something you would naturally know

Sometimes, you may get a whisper from God that is so strange, you just know this is not something you would come up with on your own. The whisper is not something that you would know in the natural, and when that happens to me, I pay attention. One time I was praying for a long line of people at a conference in southern California, and as I was praying, I looked up and saw a beautiful woman with a smile on her face, and I was stunned when I had a picture of the ugly word "betrayal" written on her forehead. Soon, she asked me for prayer because her back was hurting. To get more information about her situation, I asked her,

"When did your back start hurting?" She looked at me, and the smile disappeared from her face as she said,

"The day my husband told me he was having an affair and left me." I told her about the word I saw written on her head, and she dissolved in tears, telling me,

"Betrayal is the main feeling I feel all the time." We prayed and God healed not only her back, but also the wound of betrayal in her heart.

5 · It happens in a "thin place"

Some Christians refer to certain places where they experience God speaking in a clearer way, and often you will hear people call these "thin places," where the window between heaven and earth becomes thin, and it is as if there is an open window to heaven. Perhaps it is inside a church, or Christian retreat center, or in a place bathed with prayer (my team says ministering at the Hawaiian Islands Ministries conference is like standing under a waterfall of the Holy Spirit because there are 5,000 Christians praying in the same place).

We hear God more clearly in these places. A thin place can be a physical place for us or even seasons of time in our life. For example, I have a bench in Stanley Park in Vancouver that is a thin place for me. I have prayed there for over 18 years. Each time I go, God shows up in power. It was there that I heard my call to preach, plant a new church, write books, and have children. It is my special place with Jesus.

Thankfully, I do not have to go to Vancouver every time I want to hear God. Filoli Gardens is down the road from me, and I go there to seek God in prayer on my Sabbath days. Worship itself is a thin place for me. For Ben, nature is the thin place where he hears God, and he returns to San Gregorio beach often where God has spoken to him about critical decisions in his life. Do you have thin places where you seek God and hear Him whisper? If not, we are going to talk about that in the next chapter. God wants some thin places for you to hear Him more clearly.

6 · Confirmed with Scripture

This is different from the "consistent with Scripture" confirmation from my point number one above. Very often, God has confirmed various words, dreams, visions, or prophecies by telling me to turn to a specific verse in the Bible. The Lord is very kind to bear with my lack of faith and need for signs to know it is really Him. If I get a word, impression, or picture that I am not sure is from Him, I ask Him to confirm it. Sometimes, I will see a faint picture of Jesus flipping pages of the Bible, and pointing to a certain verse. Other times, a verse will just pop into my head. As Ben says,

"I trust those words especially, because Christy never remembers a Scripture verse on her own!" (Pretty funny considering I am a preacher and master of divinity! But I could preach a whole sermon on a certain Scripture, but forget the actual Bible verse a day later.) So, when God says, *Turn to Romans 4:18*, as he did about having children, I listen. It is a common way God speaks to me, and I know other friends who have had the same experience.

7 · "Chicken skin"

My friends in Hawaii have a funny way to describe having the chills—they just call it "chicken skin." Those are the times when you hear something or sense it is from God, and at the same time, your skin will literally feel like it has sudden goose bumps, and it is not even cold in the room! Maybe it is because I am a sleep-deprived mom, but God has started speaking a lot to me that way now. I think it is because it is hard to get my attention, so this is His way of saying, *Pay attention to this one, Christy, I'm trying to say something to you through it.*

There are other physical confirmations as well. Sometimes, when friends accompany me on trips to the emergency room to pray over patients (which some of them might tell you is a trick of mine to get them to experience God),

I will invite them to put their hands on the person while I pray. Usually, they go along with it, willing to be a source of comfort. Often, what I find is they will have some kind of experience where they sense God's presence physically, like a warm sensation on their hands.

One of my best friends, Cindy, (who would definitely say she was tricked into coming along to a healing conference once), experienced God physically herself at that very conference. After I finished speaking at the seminar, my teams lined up to pray for people. It was a larger crowd and about 50 people lined up for prayer. One woman came up for prayer who was struggling with infertility (a struggle Cindy shared with her), and my prayer team leader, Kim, dragged Cindy over to pray for her. Kim asked Cindy to put her hand on the woman's shoulder, and once she did, Cindy's legs began shaking. *What in the heck is happening?* Cindy mouthed. Kim responded plainly,

"Oh, that's just the Holy Spirit." We were thrilled to report to Cindy a month later that the woman she had prayed for got pregnant. Stuff happens. Sometimes it is physical and a bit strange, but if we are familiar with the physical signs—even the "chicken skin—we can let them stir us to faith and confidence in knowing He is speaking or moving.

8 · Confirmed through another person

You probably have people in your life that you trust love you, perhaps it is a pastor, good friend, or family member. But when they speak, it is as if God is speaking through them. When they talk, you really feel God is speaking. Possibly it is sitting in a church service, and when the pastor preaches, you feel like God is reading your mail: The sermon was, apparently, designed just for you.

9 · Happens in your heart language

What is your heart language? Is it through worship, Bible study, your intuition, your mind, art, music, or nature? God knows the language of your heart, what moves and speaks to you, and He will attempt to get messages through to you in the ways that best speak to your heart. When those God whispers come in your heart language, that is a good sign that it might be God speaking in a unique language He knows you will understand. James 3:17 says, "But the wisdom that comes from heaven is first of all pure; then peace-loving, considerate, submissive, full of mercy and good fruit, impartial and sincere," and wisdom that comes from your heart language seems to fit this description perfectly.

10 · Causes you to experience God's love more

The whole reason God whispers to His people is to show them He is there and loves them. Consequently, one sign that a whisper is from God is when you hear it, you feel the love of God. As we hear God whisper, we become more in touch with the biblical truth that God loves us more than we ever dreamed possible. We begin to experience God speaking to us in new ways that show us He cares about the things that are waking us up in the middle of the night. When that happens, our relationship with Jesus grows stronger and more intimate.

The God Whisper Scale

I developed what I call a God Whisper Scale to help myself and others categorize the level in which we have heard something from God.

The God Whisper Scale

1	2	3	4	5	6	7	8	9	10

Very faint sense, impression or word that I'm thinking actually might just be me	A stronger word that seems to me like God may be showing me this gut feeling, word or picture	A loud whisper, almost a shout from Heaven that gets my attention

The whisper scale helps me discern how much attention to give to the things I am hearing or seeing, and also what to pray about more. Having said that, I need you to know that most of the words I hear are at a level two or three. I have simply learned to pay attention, to write them down, and to risk looking like an idiot by sharing them with others. It is only when you share them that you can really determine whether it is God or not. It takes courage, but it is well worth the risk. Remember this: Even if I get a level 10 message, I always share it with humility, prefacing it this way: "I think God may have shown me something for you? May I share it?"

Finally, let me encourage you by saying that a humble heart that longs to hear God is a good thing. If you are longing to hear God's voice and willing to submit what you are hearing to the tests above, you are headed in a direction away from "bad pizza" words! Know that the Lord is with you, and He will give you discernment about His whispering voice. Remember, the Holy Spirit is on your side, and God wants to help you not only have the gift of hearing His whispers, but the gift of interpretation and discernment to test them.

GOD, PLEASE WHISPER TO ME NOW...

When it comes to hearing God's voice more, what is your greatest fear?

Has there ever been a time in your life when you think you have heard God in some way? Was it through a gut feeling? A dream? A word for someone? Write that experience down here, and then look at the God Whisper Scale above and rank it 1-10 in how strongly you sense it was from God. Why did you put that number down? What filters did you use in trying to figure out if it was from God?

Are there new ways of hearing God that you wish He would give you? A gift of pictures, words, gut feelings, chicken skin, dreams, etc. Are there other ways you can think of? Write them down, and ask God to give you that gift or another. Have your small group pray for you about it!

10

Night Whispers: Hearing God Through Dreams

And having been warned in a dream not to go back to their country,
the three wise men returned by another route.
Matthew 2:12

And afterward, I will pour out my Spirit on all people. Your sons
and daughters will prophesy, your old men will dream dreams, your
young men will see visions. Even on my servants, both men and
women, I will pour out my Spirit in those days.
Joel 2:28-29

Hot, sweaty, and eating cheese grits in Mississippi during 95-degree weather is not my idea of a good time. It was one of those sizzling hot summer days in the deep south that my brother-in-law describes perfectly as a day where "you could fry up your bacon, eggs, and grits right there on the sidewalk." We were sitting in a greasy country kitchen diner, with my new friend, Sara, eating cheese grits and drinking sweet tea. How did I end up here? Good question.

It all began at a church conference where Ben and I were both speaking. After the lecture, this woman came up to us, and honest to God, I could barely understand her she was talking so fast (not to mention her Southern accent was so strong it was almost an unintelligible other language).

"Christy, y'all just did SUCH a greeaaat job up there! I just haaave to have y'all come over to visit right now. I'll buy ya some cheese grits and sweet tea, and let me tell you about my dream 'cuz I'm thinking you might know what it means!" It was either the heat or the fact that her sentences all ran together, but I accepted her offer for cheese grits and sweet tea. So, we ended up on this hot summer day eating breakfast at the local diner with Sara.

After breakfast, Sara took us outside to the railroad tracks that crossed the highway, and with the hot sun beating down on us, she said to me,

"Christy, now I know y'all are hot, but we gotta stand right here," she said, making huge motions with her hands, "because it's the exact place I was standing in my dream, when these huge storm clouds began coming up this highway." She made more motions to wherever, I supposed, the highway was. "And then there were hundreds of people walking up the highway, with storm clouds following them. They kept coming and coming, and then next thing I see is that I'm taking these people somewhere. The people keep coming, and coming, from the South right up this highway."

At this point, I was thinking my brother-in-law was correct, it was literally so hot I could take an egg out and fry it right on the ground and eat it, but I kept trying to concentrate. "Then," she continued, "I take these people by the hand, and lead them into my grandmother's house, and I feed them! What in the world does that mean?" she exclaimed, breathless. Absolutely nothing came to my mind. I stood there with a blank face and said,

"Sara, I'm sorry. But, I have no clue what that dream means. But if God shows me something, you'll be the first person I'll call." Honestly, I was hot as blue blazes and wondered if this was one of those "bad pizza" whispers. We flew home to California the next day, and I forgot all about it.

Three months later, though, God revealed the mystery of Sara's dream. Sitting in Starbucks writing a sermon, my cell phone rings. It was my Southern friend, Sara, and she was talking a mile a minute, practically shouting at me, "Christy! Christy! It's HAPPENING! The people are coming up the highway RIGHT NOW! Hurricane Katrina hit New Orleans yesterday, and the people are streaming up here." I could not believe it. The image made so much sense now. Sara continued, "And Christy, it's so sad. They've lost everything. BUT JUST GUESS, GUESS where we set up the emergency shelter for food and clothes? My GRANDMOTHER'S HOUSE!"

Stunned, I hung up the phone. Then, I was overcome with a sense of deep gratitude to Jesus for Sara and her gift of dreams. How amazing that the Holy Spirit would give that prophetic dream to my friend, and then prepare her heart for what was to come. Over the next few months, Sara and her family managed to run a crisis shelter for Hurricane Katrina victims, and they helped hundreds of people through that terrible tragedy. Sara has become a dear friend, and I have learned so much from her about how God speaks to people in dreams.

God does whisper to His people through dreams in the night. It is a beautiful, wonderful way in which the Spirit of God communicates to people as they sleep. In fact, the Bible is filled with stories of God speaking to people through dreams. God has not stopped whispering to his people at night, and dreams remain a very common way in which the Spirit of God speaks to His children. Understanding and interpreting dreams can be tricky, though. This chapter is devoted to helping you understand dreams better and recognize the various types of dreams you might encounter personally or through another individual.

Before I was a pastor, my plan was to become a psychologist, and I had planned to do my Ph.D. in clinical psychology at Stanford University. I worked at a clinical counseling center, and frequently my clients would tell me their dreams. At that time, I always interpreted them through a clinical lens. I would tell my clients,

"Dreams are a reflection of the unconscious mind. Most of the time those dreams are showing you what your true feelings are right now in your life, but they are repressed in the daytime." In other words, dreams (in my definition) were only a mirror into your real feelings and soul.

That was my view of dreams until the day my friend, Sharon, showed up at my house with a book on dreams and told me, a bit boldly I might say, that God was going to start speaking to me in dreams. Secretly, I hoped she was wrong because I was pregnant and exhausted, and it seemed to me I needed undisturbed sleep. That night, though, I went to sleep and had what I now classify as a "God dream": The dream with Scott and I starting a ministry called "Eagles Nest." I woke up and knew Sharon had been right. I could not fit this dream so nicely into my clinical dream interpretation model (it was certainly not a secret wish of mine!). So, I began reading every book I could find on how God speaks to people through dreams.

That Eagles Nest dream was a springboard into a long journey of dream ministry. Over the past 10 years, God has taught me a lot about dreams. In my experience, I have found that there are three different kinds of dreams that I classify in this way:

1 · **God dreams**
2 · **Me dreams**
3 · **Enemy dreams**

I am going to explain these different types of dreams and give you some examples of each. One interesting thing I have found, however, is that God can use all three types of dreams in our lives, regardless of the source. It helps to know what category a dream might fall under, though, and then carefully discern its meaning.

1 · God Dreams: Dreams given to a person by the Holy Spirit that give direction, instructions, or other special divine communication

One of the coolest God dreams I have ever heard came from my friend, Vern, who lives in Hawaii. God whispers to Vern in the night through dreams very frequently now. However, Vern did not always realize that was true until she had her first big God dream.

She had moved to Honolulu and she started attending a ministry called Nightlife. Not long after that, Vern began to have very disturbing dreams about young girls being used as sex slaves. These dreams continued for almost two years, and they were graphic dreams of human trafficking that involved men, women and children. In the dreams, she would sometimes see the parents of these lost girls weeping for them, and even more disturbing, see the girls through the eyes of their pimps and abusers. Vern thought she was going crazy and told no one about the dreams for a long time because she felt something must be wrong with her to be seeing the things she saw.

Finally, she told her pastor, Jordan Seng, and he told her she was not, in fact, going crazy and that she should ask God what the dreams meant. Vern followed Jordan's advice and asked God, but His answer stunned her: *This is what happens to my children.* Feeling overwhelmed and helpless, Vern cried out to God, *Lord, why? Why in the world are you showing me?*

She felt his reply was simply, *Because if you knew, you would do something.*

Feeling completely inadequate, Vern began hanging out at midnight on the streets of Waikiki watching the prostitutes. Soon, she befriended the girls, and invited them to Bible studies. Not long after that, Vern began rescuing these girls and ministering to them. Vern is now the director of the justice ministry at Bluewater Mission. God is doing miraculous work through Vern because she listened, and responded, to the Lord after He whispered to her in a dream.

Vern's story is certainly an inspiring one. But, it began with a few elements common to God speaking through dreams: a dream and an interpretation. One of the reasons I believe God speaks to people today through dreams is that it is easier to get through to us with night whispers, than in the daytime. Think about it. We are all so dang busy and distracted! The Lord practically needs to shout through a God-sized megaphone to get our attention amidst all the calls, texts, responsibilities, children, friends, and calendar alerts.

I am guessing that many days the Lord is trying to whisper to me, but I am too busy driving for the kids' carpool, texting my friends, calling the pediatrician because a someone has strep throat, shouting at the puppy who just peed on my carpet—the list is endless. It is so loud every day that hearing God whisper is a miracle in and of itself. Consequently, I pray for God dreams. I find it extremely kind of Jesus to speak to me through night whispers because it is sometimes the only quiet time where He can get through to me.

The Bible is filled with stories of God speaking to people through dreams. In Genesis 37:5-11, we see the first of two important dreams God gave to Joseph:

> One night Joseph had a dream, and when he told his brothers about it, they hated him more than ever. "Listen to this dream," he said. "We were out in the field, tying up bundles of grain. Suddenly my bundle stood up, and your bundles all gathered around and bowed low before mine!" His brothers responded, "So you think you will be our king, do you? Do you actually think you will reign over us?" And then they hated him more than ever because of his dreams and the way he talked about them. Soon Joseph had another dream, and again he told his brothers about it. "Listen, I have had another dream," he said. "The sun, moon, and eleven stars bowed low before me!" This time he told

the dream to his father as well as to his brothers, but his father scolded him. "What kind of dream is that?" he asked. "Will your mother and I and your brothers actually come and bow to the ground before you?" But while his brothers were jealous of Joseph, his father wondered what his dreams meant.

This is an excellent example of a God dream. Notice that the dreams are symbolic, complicated, and hard to understand without divine interpretation. In fact, Joseph himself does not understand them at first. We are told, too, that his father "wonders what the dreams are about." It is not until later in life that we see these prophetic dreams fully realized when Joseph's brothers come and bow at his feet after having sold him into a life of slavery. There are so many examples of God-given dreams in the Bible that a book could be written about them alone.

God warned the three wise men in a dream not to go back the way they came to Bethlehem, to ensure that Herod did not know where Jesus was (Matthew 2:12). Daniel was a great interpreter of dreams and was repeatedly brought before kings to unravel the mysteries of dreams (Daniel 2). One of the things that Daniel makes clear to the King is that no one can interpret a dream without God's power.

Then Daniel went to Arioch, whom the king had appointed to execute the wise men of Babylon, and said to him, "Do not execute the wise men of Babylon. Take me to the king, and I will interpret his dream for him." Arioch took Daniel to the king at once and said, "I have found a man among the exiles from Judah who can tell the king what his dream means." The king asked Daniel (also called Belteshazzar), "Are you able to tell me what I saw in my dream and interpret it?" Daniel replied, "No wise man, enchanter, magician or diviner can explain to the king the mystery he has asked about, but there is a God in heaven who reveals mysteries." (Daniel 2:24-28)

Those are just a few examples of dreams in the Bible, but if you read your Bible, cover to cover, you will see that God speaks to people in dreams quite often. One of the things I would encourage you to do if you already hear God in dreams is to spend time researching the Bible stories where God spoke to people in their dreams.

2 · Me dreams: Dreams that are more likely to be a reflection of your own feelings and soul

Dreams are typically symbolic, and it takes some experience to learn to interpret them. Therefore, you need wisdom, discernment, and interpretation before you decide what the dream really means. The fun thing about this is that it often takes a team approach in decoding a God dream, which means more people get to share in the joy of God whispering. A Me dream (the definition of which my kids and I worked on together) typically reflects how you are feeling about someone or something in your own personal life. For example, Corey came downstairs one morning and said,

"Mom, I have a science test today, and I had this wacky dream that my science teacher handed me a test with a huge red letter 'F' written on it." That was a very clear example of a Me dream. Corey is an A student, but struggles with being a perfectionist and can be a worrier. She was able to interpret that one right away: Her fears were finding a voice in her dream.

Interestingly, though, God can use all our dreams to help us. Me dreams can be used by God to help us discover how we really feel about certain things. In Corey's case, this Me dream was a great opportunity to see more clearly feelings she did not know were deep inside her. We took that opportunity to pray over breakfast for Corey's test, but also for God to lift those worries and give her peace.

As an aside, there are many good clinical books you can read about how to interpret dreams from a psychological worldview. While I have done counseling in a clinical setting and learned a lot from good doctors on this process, I am not an expert. If you are interested in understanding how dreams are a reflection of the unconscious at times, I would recommend finding a good Christian therapist who is experienced in both psychological dream interpretation as well as in understanding Divine communication in dreams.

3 · Enemy dreams: Dreams that are sent from Satan or demons to harass us in the night

These types of dreams are sometimes called "warfare dreams." While Enemy dreams are not my favorite kind of nighttime whisper, it is often a good thing when they happen because they help me see clearly that I am under some kind of spiritual attack. When that happens, the Enemy's plans are exposed, and it shows me how to pray.

Both of my girls have the gift of dreams. We regularly interpret our dreams and learn from God together. Annie has a special gift of discernment and will often be a spiritual barometer when it comes to spiritual attack. When she has an Enemy dream, she has learned not to be scared, but actually somewhat encouraged, because we discover together where the Enemy is harassing us. Then, we know how to pray against the attacks, and God sends His peace.

Not long ago, Annie had a significant dream about our city. In the dream, a man who looked like Willy Wonka came to Annie and Corey at their middle school. The man held out money and said, *Annie and Corey, if you follow me, I'll give you all the money in the world. Then I can give you all the power in the world. And, I can make you like God, too.* In the dream, Annie and Corey realize that he is not a nice man, but evil, and he was trying to capture them and take them into his car. Just in time, Ben and I show up and rescue them. God showed me that the Willy Wonka character in Annie's dream is actually a principality (a spiritual stronghold) and power over our area. Interestingly, this demonic spirit's mission over the people in our town is the same one: to deceive people into thinking that what matters is money, power, and being their own god. This spirit disguises itself as a giver of happiness, but the all-too-common result in pursuing those things alone is emptiness, meaningless living, destruction of relationships and even in some cases, death.

My friend, Gary, is the senior pastor of Peninsula Covenant Church, and has a cool story about Enemy dreams. He has five girls now, and one night every member of the family had the same bad dream about an intruder coming into the house. When they compared dreams in the morning, they understood clearly that they were under spiritual attack. It was pretty stupid of the Enemy, I would say, because it rallied the troops, so to speak, and got the church praying over the house. And then there was peaceful sleep!

Dream interpretation: How to become a dream detective

While the Bible is full of stories of normal people having God dreams, it is also evident that the correct interpretation of dreams is a very important part of the dream process. Dream interpretation can be a bit tricky, but it is well worth the effort to seek God's wisdom to interpret your dreams. My son, Benji, puts it like this,

"Mom, it's actually pretty fun decoding our dreams. It's kind of like we are dream detectives figuring out a mystery together." Leave it to my all-boy, Benji, to make an action game out of dream interpretation. Benji is right though. It really is fun to decode dreams. I want to end this chapter by giving you some general guidelines for how to interpret dreams.

Since dreams are rarely strictly literal, they are more often filled with symbols and codes. Still, it is worth the effort to analyze them. Here are a few clues in your dream detective work:

Ask God!

Probably the most helpful advice I can give you is simply this: Ask the Lord what your dream means. Give it to Him, pray, and ask the Lord to give you insight and wisdom. Sometimes God will give you the dream again, and it will make more sense.

Start a dream journal:

Keep a journal, light, and pencil by your bedside. Write down your dreams when you wake—even if it is still the middle of the night.

Read stories from the Bible:

Read about God speaking to people in dreams. Both the Old and the New Testament have tons of stories!

Learn from gifted dreamers:

Learn what Jesus has taught them, and reflect on their wisdom in your own journey.

Teaching your kids about dreams

One of my greatest joys in life is seeing how Jesus speaks to my kids through the Holy Spirit, and "training them up" in the way they should go about knowing Him (Proverbs 22:6). Both Corey and Annie, our little dreamers, have experienced God speak to them about something for our ministry. We have a great time trying to decode dreams. Corey's dreams are so complex and long that Ben teases her that he has got to get a big cup of coffee before she gets started telling us her dream because it may go on for awhile.

My kids find it extremely comforting and empowering to know that they have God's power to stand against the Enemy. Almost every night they will say, "Mom, did you pray over our dreams?" When they do have a nightmare, they are actually relieved as we talk through its possible meanings and realize it was just an Enemy dream. Annie will usually say something like,

"Co, that's just the Enemy messing with you. Now we know to step up the prayers." Interestingly, many secular therapists will counsel parents to tell their children that they have "magic powers" to send away bad dreams. As Christians, we do not need any fake or magic power because we have the real power of the Holy Spirit to fight against the Enemy (Ephesians 6:12-17).

Consequently, teaching our kids how to war in the Spirit is one of the most caring parental things we can do. In our house, if we are having bad dreams, we anoint the room with oil, play worship music very quietly in the room at night (demons hate worship music), pray over our dreams, ask the Lord to take our minds captive to Christ, and forbid the Enemy from giving us bad dreams. Some parents ask what to do when that does not work. Most of the time, I find parents who take this approach actually have wonderful experiences of their children having amazing God dreams. Their children also report feeling safer at night because of they prayed away the "bad spirits." One of our favorite nighttime prayers goes like this (and you are welcome to use any of it that might help your kids!):

Lord, we pray for good dreams, for God dreams, and for you to watch over us as we sleep. We ask you to send your angels by the hundreds to surround our house tonight. Holy Spirit, we ask you to speak to us through dreams, and we forbid the Enemy from giving us any bad dreams. In Jesus' name, Amen.

GOD, PLEASE WHISPER TO ME NOW...

Do you remember a dream that might possibly fall in the God Dream category?

Can you think of examples of Me dreams or Enemy dreams that you or someone you know have experienced?

What kinds of tools mentioned above in the "dream detective" section might be helpful to you?

PRAYER

God, thank you that you speak to people through dreams. I ask that you would use my dreams, however you wish, to speak to me as I sleep. Whisper to me at night in ways that make sense to me. In Jesus' name I pray, Amen.

11

Big Ears

But Jesus often withdrew to lonely places and prayed.
Luke 5:16

Let us be silent, that we may hear the whisper of God.
Ralph Waldo Emerson

I saw Pam Chun with elephant ears. Seriously. As I looked out into the audience at a conference where I was speaking, I saw a picture of Pam Chun, a dear friend and co-founder of Hawaiian Islands Ministries in Hawaii, with huge cartoon elephant ears. As I was stifling my laughter, I heard God whisper to me, *Tell Pam she has big ears and they're about to get bigger.* (I know, what the heck, right? Sometimes you really DO think you have eaten spicy pizza!)

In fact, I have a tendency to want to move on, to blow off these strange impressions, because I may be wrong or I do not want to look weird. Over time, though, I have learned to take some risks, and humbly share these impressions, because God has repeatedly shown me that He is often speaking through me to other people. God really does have a sense of humor, and I am always amazed at the coded messages He often whispers to me. Maybe it is because He knows I am so tired from my life as a mom and pastor, but God knows He has to be really creative to get my attention!

Regardless, it is not unusual for me to see or to hear things I do not understand at all, and it requires me stepping out in faith and asking people about them. Otherwise, I will never know if it is God or the spicy pizza thing! More importantly, I do not want to miss the opportunity to share something that will really minister to someone just because I thought it was nothing.

I cannot tell you the number of times I almost did not share a word with someone because it was just a level two or three on the God Whisper Scale (from chapter nine), but did anyway. Later, I am so thankful that I did not hold back, because it was a life-changing moment when that person heard God's voice in an extraordinary way.

That night, I knew Pam would get a kick out of this picture, and so I ran and found her after my session and told her what I saw. I also told her that my sense was it was God's funny way of showing us ahead of time that He was about to increase her ability to hear Him more. That interpretation turned out to be true, for her ability to hear His voice began to grow stronger and stronger in the months ahead. God was giving her big ears to hear His Spirit speaking to her in ways she had not yet experienced in her life.

We all need bigger ears. It does not matter how much experience you have had with hearing God speak. Whether you hear God a lot, or very little, or do not think you hear Him at all, know this: God *wants* to give you bigger ears. The heart of your Father in Heaven for you is so beautifully epitomized in Jeremiah 33:3: "Call to me and I will answer you, and teach you great and unsearchable things you do not yet know." God does not want you to be disappointed in your journey of trying to hear His voice. Instead, Jesus wants to put His arm around you, whisper God-messages into your ear, and constantly communicate to you that you are deeply loved.

How do we develop bigger ears to hear the Spirit of God? Hearing God is a lifelong journey, and usually it does not happen overnight. At the same time, I am convinced that God longs to get your attention way more than you may realize, and He has specific, encouraging, loving things to speak to you.

In this chapter, I am going to share some very practical ways to experience God speaking that I am hoping will increase the volume in your prayer life. As you read, I would invite you to "chew up the fish, spit out the bones," as Ben would say. Some of the following tools will help you develop bigger ears in your relationship with God, while others might be helpful for someone else.

1 · Do what Jesus did to hear the Father's voice

If you read the New Testament, you will notice that Jesus was crystal clear on His mission from the Father. Like a laser beam, He is focused on doing exactly what the Father shows Him to do and leaves aside the things He is not to do. In fact, Jesus says, "I tell you the truth, the Son can do nothing by himself; He can do only what he sees his Father doing" (John 5:19).

As a pastor, I am often overwhelmed by the endless needs around me, and it is difficult to discern which ministry is the most important. I am always amazed at how Jesus seemed to reach out to some individuals, but did not heal everyone there. On Good Friday, we watch in both horror and awe as this man without sin, allowed himself to be whipped, beaten, spit on, and crucified for our sins. He gave his own life to save us from our sins, and give us eternal life forever.

Because of what Jesus did, you and I have the right to an intimate relationship with the Father, through the Holy Spirit, so that we can draw near to Him and hear His voice as children of God (1 John 1:12). Jesus was able to fulfill His mission in life, because He was listening closely to the Father for his moment-to-moment marching orders.

So, just how did Jesus do that? The answer becomes clear in Scripture when we see over and over again that Jesus spent hours alone with the Father. Luke 5:16 says, "He often withdrew to quiet and lonely places." Before Jesus had the power to do his ministry on this earth, He went to the wilderness for 40 days to be with His Father. After his wilderness experience, He returned "in the power of the Holy Spirit" (Luke 4:14). Finally, before the hardest moment of his time on earth, Jesus fell to his knees in the Garden of Gethsemane, crying out to the Father, "Lord if it's possible, let this cup pass from me, but not my will be done, Thy will be done" (Luke 22:42). After spending that time alone with His Father in the wilderness, Jesus emerged strong and ready for his ministry. Before the most trying sacrifice any man could ever give, Jesus knelt in the Garden alone before His Father.

So, ask yourself this question: If Jesus (who was, by the way, fully God and fully man) needed to have that time alone with God, how much more do you and I need to withdraw from our chaotic lives to be with the Lord in prayer? If Jesus needed to withdraw from the crowds to hear the Father speak to Him, in a culture where there were no cell phones, computers, e-mails, or texts beeping, how much more do we need to find quiet places to seek God?

2 · Whatever it takes, whatever it costs, find quiet places to hear God whisper

Every time I get into the practical issues of how to hear God more clearly, I feel guilty. I look out at people, and I know how weary they are by their stressful lives. They are tired. Many are working long hours trying to make ends meet. Haggard business executives, exhausted parents, stressed students: They are all pulled in so many directions. Even now, I think to myself, *Life is already overwhelming for them, and the last thing I want to do is put another thing on their to-do list!*

Hearing God's voice should be a joy, not a guilt trip! At the same time, I have come to realize that it is not kind or pastoral to sugarcoat the truth. In order to hear God more, you must be intentional about seeking Him. This is especially true if you have not had a lot of prior experience in hearing God's voice through the Holy Spirit in some of these new ways. It is not a news flash that this is extremely challenging. Think about it: Can God speak to you very clear, intimate messages that breathe life and direction into your soul while you are driving a carpool of screaming kids, talking on your cellphone, and drinking a latte? Well, He is God, it is certainly possible. However, there is a way better chance you are going to develop a more conversational relationship with Jesus if you are intentional about developing listening ears by trying some new things in your prayer life.

One of Satan's major attack plans for your life is to keep you so busy and distracted that you will not make time to seek God. He wants you so busy that you never stop to hear His voice. The Enemy is not stupid. He knows that the very best way to keep you discouraged, depressed, stressed out, confused about your destiny in Jesus, and just plain worn out, is to keep you so frantically busy so you will not stop to hear the quiet whispers of Jesus. I know because I do it all the time. I forget that God is waiting, following me around, longing for me to stop, for just a moment, so that I can hear His quiet whisper into my ears that will breathe hope, peace, healing, and new direction in my life.

For me, this means that I must be ruthless about seeking God. I must find a quiet place in my home. I actually put up a door on the entrance to our living room, which I now can shut when I am in there praying. Otherwise, I would be distracted by the puppy fighting with the cat, my kids yelling for breakfast or someone saying, "Mom I need…" Those of you who have kids know exactly what I mean. Will my door stop the endless flow of demands? No, but it helps shut out the noise for a bit. (As I wrote that, my puppy just climbed up on my lap and threw up.) I have to literally shut the door in my house to tune out other voices and tune into God's voice.

Better yet, I need to escape to a quiet and lonely place outside my home. You may find that your home is not an ideal place to seek God. People at work might be calling you, or your computer sitting on the kitchen table might be tempting you—any number of things. Despite my quiet room, with the door closed, I can get distracted in my home by my endless to-do list, so I have to withdraw weekly to a longer time with Jesus in a quiet place. I go to Filoli Gardens and spend several hours quieting the noise in my brain walking and talking with God. My daughter Corey, the teenager, gets overwhelmed with the noise of Snapchat, Instagram, texts, and e-mails, and she literally begs me to go to Filoli so she can walk in nature and just be with God. People in her generation are desperate for real encounters with Jesus where they hear His voice for themselves.

In our family, we are getting very serious about Sabbath in our home. Frequently, my kids and I will go to a quiet place in nature, with our Bibles and journals. We are learning to hear God together. It is a wonderful, precious time, and I am blown away at how my kids are learning to hear God for themselves. Where are your quiet places? Is it at home in a special chair? Do you need to escape your home and find a quiet bench in a park? Are you like me and you need your worship music? Whatever it takes, whatever it costs, withdraw often like Jesus did, to hear God speak into your life.

3 · Try

My friend, Jordan Seng, the senior pastor at Bluewater Mission, leads a revolutionary movement to simplicity in following God with the church's mission statement: Try. (Just three letters! Is that not great?) By that little three-letter mission statement, they make it normal to step out in faith trusting God to show up. It is a safe place to try, knowing it is also OK to fail. They trust that if we have humble hearts trying to do what Jesus has invited us to do, He will show up.

Probably the most practical thing I can encourage you to do in your own journey of seeking to hear God more is the same message: Try. Choose to believe, as the Bible tells you, that God loves you more than you can possibly imagine, and that He cares about the things that you are worried about. Choose to believe, that God wants to give you bigger ears, if you will only give Him half a chance. Be willing to try new things to hear God more. Ask God for dreams, words of knowledge, prophetic words, visions, new things that you have not experienced before.

4 · Ask God to turn up the volume!

Once you are hanging out with God in some quiet place, ask God to turn up the volume. Remember the Scripture that says, "If you then, though you are evil, know how to give good gifts to your children, how much more will your Father in heaven give the Holy Spirit to those who ask him…" (Luke 11:13)? Asking God to speak louder into your life is a prayer that God will answer. It may take longer than you think. It may take some practice, but if you seek God and yearn to hear His voice, you will start to experience Him whispering more loudly than you did before.

5 · Press the mute button on Satan

In order to turn up the volume on God's voice, you must learn to silence the other voices in your mind. As a friend of mine says, each of us has at least one lie we believe about ourselves. Please prayerfully think about this: What are the voices inside your mind saying to you? Are they building you up or tearing you down? Maybe the messages sound like, *You are God's special kid! You are beautiful and dearly loved! You CAN do all things through Christ who strengthens you! Do not be afraid, for I am right here with you and I will give you everything you need.* Are you hearing those things? Or are you hearing other messages?

Please take some time, and write down the messages you hear most in your own mind. Then, please find a good Christian friend, or even a counselor, and figure out where those messages are coming from. What are the lies you believe about yourself? I remember one day Corey said to me,

"Mom, I think Satan might be lying to me, can you pray for me?" Of course the Mama Bear in me got very mad at the Enemy and asked,

"Corey, what are you hearing?" She responded simply,

"The Enemy is saying that I should be afraid because he is going to kill the people that matter to me." The Mama Bear was on the offensive now. We are told in Scripture that the Enemy "comes only to steal and kill and destroy" (John 10:10)—and that Satan is a liar. I am thankful that Corey knew to recognize the voice of the Enemy and to come to someone she trusted to pray. Together, we prayed against that lie. I pray the following prayer regularly over my kids:

In the name of Jesus, I command the lying voice of the Enemy to be silent. In the name of Jesus, I declare you off-limits to the Enemy! I put the helmet of salvation over your head, and I say that only God's good messages can come through to your mind. I pray that God would give you a gift of discernment so you can recognize the lies of the enemy when they come and tell the enemy this: SHUT UP in Jesus' name!

That moment with Corey was a wonderful moment of pushing the mute button on the Enemy. Please prayerfully reflect on the voices you are hearing. Most likely, you need to press the mute button on some lies Satan is whispering to you. You also may discover some "old tapes" of negative messages from your past that people have said to you that also need to be destroyed. Ask friends or a good Christian counselor to help bring into the light those lies and silence them in Jesus' name.

6 · Put together an emergency "whisper bag"

In California, we are supposed to have emergency bags in our cars, houses, and workplaces in case of earthquakes. I am told that these should include non-perishable goods, cash, bottled water, extra clothing, and a first aid kit. (Honest confession: The Pierce family is not well prepared just yet!) After Hurricane Sandy, we are getting more serious about our emergency supplies, and we have now have a generator in our shed, canned goods, and water in our garage.

Those are preparations for our physical well-being, so why should we not also prepare for our spiritual well-being? Our "whisper bags" (as we call them)

include a Bible, journal, worship music, and snacks. We carry them around in our car, because more often than not, our plans for quiet times with God will get derailed because of sick kids or an emergency pastoral hospital visit. We are ready, however, to grab some moments to be with God in the middle of our chaotic life. I am truly amazed at how compassionate God is regarding our crazy schedules. Sometimes, I will pull the minivan over on the road if I have got a few minutes before picking up kids, pop in my worship CD, and read the Bible. I ask God to speak to me in these few minutes I have. Frequently, He does. Jesus longs to get our attention, even if we only have a few minutes, and He delights in showing up in the time I do have.

7 · Take up journaling

If you have not had much experience with journaling, this is something you would be wise to try. There is actually a lot of confirmation that journaling is directly connected with people's ability to hear God's voice more clearly. What do we mean by journaling? There are various ways to journal, not one right way, but I would advocate writing down your thoughts and emotions to God. Write a letter to God, or keep a journal on your iPhone or computer or whatever you use. Tell God how you are honestly doing, honestly feeling. Vent to Him any feelings, anger (God can handle it!), sadness, or worry, and tell Him specifically where you need His help. Tell God your prayer requests, your dreams, your hopes, and your fears. Then, do what many people (including experienced Christian leaders, theologians, and pastors) often do not do: listen. The truth in our Western culture is that we are very good at talking to God but not so good at listening. One thing I encourage people to do when that get to that listening part of their prayer time with God is this: Give God a chance to speak, even if it is two minutes of closing your eyes and paying attention to what crosses your mind. You may be surprised as you see a picture, or hear a faint word, or have an impression. Write that down. Then, ask God to confirm it. Be willing to share it with other people with a humble learner's heart, so you can get discernment from others in the Body of Christ. Over time, you might find that the little, faint words you hear, the ones that you always thought were just you, are actually from God more often that you realized. Write down the whispers, then test them to see if it is God speaking or the bad piece of pizza!

8 · Test the whispers

Testing the things you are hearing from God is critical. Without discernment and wisdom, things can get wacky, imbalanced, and people can get hurt. It is really important to submit the words, dreams, impressions, and prophecies to other safe Christians who will help you discern if what you are hearing is really from God. I test God's whispers by screening what I see and hear through these filters: Is it consistent with Scripture? Did I submit it to people I trust for feedback? And, did I ask God what I should do with it? One of my colleagues, Jack Deere, is a well-known speaker and writer on how to hear God's voice. Jack has this wonderful saying about testing words from God when he says in his book, *Surprised by the Voice of God,* that there is revelation, interpretation, and application. When you think you have heard something from God, it is called revelation. When you then need to ask yourself, *What does this mean?* you need interpretation, which involves submitting it to Christians you trust. Finally, you must ask God what you are supposed to do with the word, sense, picture, or whatever else you may have sensed God say to you—that is application. Remember, not everything you hear from God is supposed to be shared. Sometimes, God is showing you something you are to hold to yourself, but confidentially pray about. That is a good thing to learn that can save you and your church a lot of pain. In fact, I want to take the next few pages to discuss that very real concern Christian leaders and pastors have when it comes to encouraging hearing God in their congregations.

Encourage your church to hear God's voice, without causing an explosion!

Having a church that is vibrant in the Holy Spirit, where hearing God speak in words, visions, dreams, and pictures is possible without blowing up your church with unmet expectations, comparison, disappointment—even fear. It makes me so sad when people become excited about hearing God's voice, and then things start to get wacky and unbalanced, and (be honest) weird! It is a huge buzz kill when a fresh wind of the Holy Spirit moves in a church, only to have someone blow it by saying something along the lines of "God told me you have the sin of lust, and you should put on sack cloth and ashes" type of thing.

A very common problem that you must be on your guard to snuff out is the spirit of pride. That very same spirit of pride is one we see in the Corinthian church in the Bible. In that church, many mistakes were happening all at once, but one of the worst involved this nasty, prideful spirit. Believers of Christ in the Corinthian church got excited about the gifts of the Spirit, but then they made the big mistake of making others feel "less than" because they themselves were not having prophetic words, dreams, or visions. That is something that Paul shut down, and we should too. Churches have split over this stuff, and there is no need for that to happen.

Here are some safeguards and rules for your church to make it a safe place to learn, but still maintain some order that keeps things balanced. Most of the blowups I have encountered as a consultant to churches wanting to move more in the ministry of the Holy Spirit could have been avoided by following the following guidelines.

1 · Do not use the words "God told me" this side of heaven

I can tell you from personal experience that when someone comes to me and says, "God told me to tell you this," I want to run. Biblically speaking, none of us are on the same level as the Old Testament prophets, who had 100 percent accuracy in hearing God because they were God's mouthpieces in that day. They could literally say "God told me" with complete confidence because God had literally told them. After Jesus came, the Holy Spirit was poured out on all believers.

At that time, the Apostle Paul said, "We now see through a mirror dimly, but one day we will see face to face" (1 Corinthians 13:12). The implication is that we will not have 100 percent accuracy in hearing God's voice. Still, the Apostle Paul urges the Corinthian church to embrace the gifts of the Spirit—especially prophecy! (I find that fact interesting, given that the spiritual gifts had caused some real damage and mess. That was just how important Paul considered the gift of prophecy, words of knowledge, visions, and the like.) God wants us to seek and respect the gift of prophecy (1 Corinthians 14:1), but tells us at the same time that we must test the spirits to know which are from God (1 John 4:1). And far from being insecure and demanding that people accept his every word as God-inspired, Paul commended the Bereans for checking what he told them against God's Word (Acts 17:11).

Consequently, I advise people to use language like, "I think God might have shared something with me for you that I think might encourage you. May I share it with you?" Or, "I believe God gave me a picture for you, and here is what I saw. But ask God yourself, for if it's the Holy Spirit, He will show you."

Now, I admit that if I am with close friends who know me well, I might not tiptoe so carefully, and blurt out a "God told me" a little more often. Also, if I am in a church culture that is more experienced in the ministry of the Holy Spirit, I might change my lingo slightly. Most of the time, though, I am ministering in churches that are strong in Bible teaching, preaching, evangelism, and missions, but the ministry of the Holy Spirit and hearing God's voice is new. I feel a pastoral responsibility to help them use language that will keep things safe.

Finally, I would strongly advise that if you humbly share a word you heard from God with another person, and they say, "That makes no sense to me" or react in a negative way, back off! It is not your responsibility to convince someone that you saw or heard something from the Holy Spirit. It is your job to share things in love, and leave it to God to confirm it. The Bible says that prophecy is for the building up of the church (1 Corinthians 14:4). (The point being, then, to build up, not tear down, obviously!). If someone tells me that the word I shared with them does not seem to connect, I back off and say, "OK, maybe I heard wrong. Thanks for letting me share it with you." Interestingly, often the person will come back later and recant his or her original hesitation, saying instead that the word was valid. God is funny that way.

2 · Do not be afraid to step out and humbly share whispers (even if they happen at Starbucks!)

Yes, you can even get whispers at Starbucks. Honestly, it is sometimes inconvenient. You are just trying to get that *venti triple latte* pick-me-up before you get kids in school and hearing God whisper was not on your to-do list. One day, I was standing in line and the barista, Scott, asked if I wanted the usual coffee. I smiled at him and responded,

"That's perfect, Scott, thanks for remembering." Standing in line, I hear God whisper the craziest thing: *Give Scott $200 and tell him it's about teeth.* I stood there blankly. Um, no way. That was a "bad pizza" whisper for sure, right? You would think I might be bold enough by now to listen to these whispers and just step out courageously each time I hear them. Wrong. Often, I am looking around for an excuse to not do anything. Sometimes, when I try to walk away, God tugs gently at my heart, and I know I need to take that risk and share it.

I called up Ben to get his permission to write the $200 check, and he tells me to go for it, because even though we both know it is not in the budget, Ben senses a tug too. Ugh! No more excuses. So, I meet Scott at the counter when my latte comes up. Here goes. "Hey Scott. Well, this might sound really crazy, but I am a pastor and sometimes God whispers to me. I think I heard God say that I'm supposed to give you $200. Something about teeth?" I stammer, getting less confident as I continue. "I hope that's OK with you, so, uh, here's a check," I said and thrust it in his hands.

Well, I am not going to lie to you. It was a little awkward. Scott started at me and tears filled his eyes (right there at the insanely busy drink hand-off point). He took the check and softly told me he needed exactly that amount to fix his teeth. Turns out Scott, only 19, was the oldest child in his family to leave Mexico and was now supporting himself and a younger sister who was in high school here in the States. He, of course, had no money to spend on a visit to the dentist.

Later, he told me that his grandmother sobbed on the phone when he called her in Mexico to tell her about the God whisper. Scott and I still keep in touch. He has become a strong Christian and is active in a local church in Redwood City. I would say that the courage I managed to muster to share the whisper was nothing when compared to the work God was able to do in my obedience and vulnerability. When we are faithful, He certainly is.

I would not necessarily consider myself a slow learner, but on this issue—boldly stepping out in faith that God speaks—I need a lot of lessons. Last summer, Ben and I were doing a Whispers of God conference in the south. Before we arrived, I spent some time on our family's farm listening to God. I have learned to jot down in my notes things I hear, and however faint the whisper might be, I repeatedly see that if I step out in faith and share these whispers, God meets people in extraordinary ways. Usually, I say something like, "OK, I'm now going to take a step of faith that God may have whispered something for you. Some of these impressions may be from God, some may be that bad piece of pizza thing we talked about where I might have heard Jesus wrong." Then I usually add, "But, I'll trust the Lord to guide us and show us what is from Him and what isn't." Then, I will invite the Holy Spirit to come and take over our prayer time, and I share the impressions or words that God has given me.

In this particular conference, I really did not have many strong impressions at all. In fact, I had written them down on a napkin with one of Benji's crayons I had found at the bottom of my messy purse. Convinced I did not have any specific messages for this crowd, I was going to simply end my session by praying for people and call it a day. God had other plans. Instead, He nudged me to look at that crayon written message on the napkin and I said,

"OK, folks, this is a faint whisper, but if it means something to you guys, I wanted to share it." Then I read the crayon note, "Someone named Sheri. Back problem. Deeper wound God wants to heal." The room gasped. Apparently, the children's minister was named Sheri, and she had a chronic back problem the church was praying for, but the bigger wound was a personal issue in her family. She came forward later in tears, so touched that God loved her enough to show a stranger she was in pain. We had a wonderful prayer time, and God did some very tender healing of her heart that day and the pain in her back disappeared.

That night, I was talking to Ben about all this whispering stuff, convicted that I almost missed that important God moment in Sheri's life because I was hesitant to share a crayon-scribbled whisper on a napkin. (You think I would know better by now, right?) Again, the quickest way you are going to figure out if you are hearing God correctly for someone else is to risk looking foolish. Share the word, even if it is only a level one on the God Whisper Scale! Share it with humility and love: "I think God may have given me this word, or picture, for you. I hope it encourages you in some way. If it's not God, forgive me for being wrong, but I didn't want to miss it if God was trying to say something uplifting to you."

3 · Use caution with "negative words" and only share them if God confirms through others you need to share it

What if the word you hear is negative in some way? For example, what if you see a picture of the word "adultery" written over a person's head? What if you sense someone is struggling with a certain sin? What if the word you hear for another person seems harsh and like it might hurt their feelings? Be careful.

Most of the time, we are called to communicate messages from God that build people up. I steer very strongly on the side of encouraging prophetic words and impressions that build people's faith and help them feel God's love. There are times, however, when God is showing us a person's sin or problems. Much of the time, God may be showing you only because you are supposed to pray for that person. If you really have a hard message, test it big time. Pray over it. Make sure it is not about you. Submit it to Christian leaders and people you trust. If you feel called to share it, do so in true humility. Give the person a chance to back out. You are not Jeremiah or Isaiah prophesying, and if God wants to convict that person of a sin or struggle, that is His job. Also, it is possible to share hard words in ways that do not reveal all of what you may be seeing, unless the person invites you into the situation further.

Once, I asked a friend to pray over a young woman who had been sexually abused. My prophetic friend knew nothing of the young woman's situation, and the victim of abuse knew she was clueless. My friend praying said gently, "Do you want to tell me anything about your situation or just pray like the Spirit leads me?" The woman opted to tell nothing. Looking over at my friend pray, I just knew she knew. But a look of tender compassion came over her face and she said, "The Lord knows what happened to you and it broke His heart. He wants you to know that you are now safe, and that what happened to you will never happen again. You are believing a lie that it was your fault, and God says it's not your fault." I watched this young woman as tears fell down her cheeks. It was a beautiful moment and I thanked God again for believers who move in the gift of prophecy.

4 · Remember that hearing "wrong" is how you grow

If you have the guts to try new things and to learn about hearing God's voice more, that is good news. The bad news, especially for those of us who are perfectionists, is this: You will hear wrong. Yep, you will. But that is also the good news. When you hear wrong, you will learn. For me, the only failure is not being willing to try. If you humbly step out trying to hear God, the benefits are way bigger than any risk of hearing wrong a few times along the way.

5 · Have a humble attitude and you will succeed

When it comes to hearing and sharing God's whisper, humility is so very important. I have found that if whispers from God are shared in humble ways with people, the result is usually one of blessing. People learn well in a safe community. We do not learn if it is really God unless we are willing to submit the whispers, pictures, experiences to the Body of Christ.

6 · Get your Ph.D. in hearing God's voice: Join a small group

Without question, the best place to learn how to hear God's voice is in Christian community. Specifically, I am talking about a small group experience. I would not have learned without it. Remember, I thought people who said God showed them a picture or they heard a word from God, were weird! I had no experience seeing this stuff in action, so my lack of experience is what formed my theology.

Until I started experiencing God speaking during a small group in Kansas City, my worldview was that God only spoke through the Bible and good sermons. After joining that small group, where all of us were rookies in hearing God through prayer, I learned I was totally wrong. One week in that group, we asked for a volunteer to pray for and ended up getting that funny word ("Cat"), which turned into a profound experience with the Holy Spirit that I talked about in chapter eight. God changed all of our opinions that day about how quietly He whispers words of compassion for those in pain. Without that small group, I would never have learned to hear Jesus speaking through the Holy Spirit in this way. Most folks I know that have a good track record when it comes to hearing God speak, which was learned through a small group of people where they could practice praying for one another. In fact, I would say if you want your Ph.D. in hearing God, let people pray for you! If you do not know of a small group that is a good laboratory to learn how to hear God more in your life, start one! Chapter 12 has some very specific guidelines about how to start and lead a small group on hearing God whisper.

7 · Hang out with people who have big ears

In addition to practicing in small groups, it will help you to hang out with people who have big ears. Read books, attend conferences, and visit area churches where hearing God's voice and sharing those impressions is their cup of tea.

(Visit our website at www.christypierce.org for some resources to help you.)

Again, I will advise you to chew up the fish, spit out the bones. Have a learner's heart! You will likely learn new things about hearing God, and then you might need to take the meat of what you discovered, and put it in your church's unique wineskin. Take your small group on a field trip to these types of churches and events, and ask God to teach you from those who have gone before you.

GOD, PLEASE WHISPER TO ME NOW...

In your personal journey to develop bigger ears to hear God, what practical ways might be most helpful to you?

Think about the following ways I suggested below, and put a check beside the ones that might help you most. You might add others that you have thought of which would be just what you need instead.

☐ Withdrawing to quiet places alone like Jesus did
☐ Whatever it takes, whatever it costs, find quiet places for me to hear God whisper more
☐ Try
☐ Ask God to turn up the volume!
☐ Press the mute button on Satan's lies
☐ Put together my own emergency "whisper bag"
☐ Buy a new journal and start journaling myself
☐ Test the whispers I hear from God
☐ Encourage my church to hear God's voice, and reassure folks we can do this stuff without causing an explosion!
☐ Get my Ph.D. in hearing God's voice, by joining a small group where it is safe to practice hearing God more

Do you still have concerns about stepping out to hear God's voice? I mentioned some "safeguards" (listed below) to keep in mind when practicing hearing God.

Do you agree or disagree with these practical guidelines? Can you think of other safe guards that will allow the flow of the Holy Spirit in hearing God but also protect people?

- Do not use the words "God told me" this side of heaven
- Share words and impressions with other safe people, even if you are not sure if it is a "bad pizza" one
- Use caution with negative words and only share them if God confirms through others you need to share it
- Remember that hearing "wrong" is how you grow
- Have a humble attitude and you will succeed

PRAYER

Lord, I want to develop bigger ears to hear your voice. Only you know the best practical things I can do to hear you more clearly, so would you guide me into the things that will help grow my faith in hearing your whispering voice? Amen.

12

Your Turn Now

And without faith, it's impossible to please God, because anyone who comes to him must believe that He exists, and that He rewards those who earnestly seek Him.

Hebrews 11:6

Hello Lord, it's me your child, I have a few things on my mind. Right now, I'm faced with big decisions, and I'm wondering if you have a minute? Cuz right now, I don't hear so well and I was wondering if you could speak up?

Sara Groves "Hello Lord"

When my son, Benji, was two years old, he would stand on top of a chair, and shout at his sisters,

"MY TURN NOW!" Looking back, it actually made a lot of sense from his point of view. His adoring sisters had bossed around this cute, blond-haired, blue-eyed boy since birth. Now, Benji wanted to do things on his own. He wanted a turn for himself.

At some point in our quest to hear God's whispers, we want to move beyond learning about how God whispers, and into experiencing God's whispering ourselves. Simply put, we want our own turn. When our desire to hear God's voice more brings us to the point where we have courage to say to the Lord, Please, God, I want a turn now, it truly brings joy to the Father's heart. It is a prayer that God promises to answer, for you are His special kid. The Bible exhorts us to press into God, and to not hold back, for "He rewards those who earnestly seek Him" (Hebrews 11:6).

We are now at an important crossroads. As I write and speak encouraging people that they can hear God talking to them directly, I am aware that anything I say is completely inadequate to a real-life encounter with the Living God. It is one thing to talk about hearing God's voice; it is a whole other deal to have Jesus turn up the volume in your own prayer life where you are getting pictures, words, visions, dreams, or fresh encounters with the Living God in ways you never dreamed possible.

Over time, I have experienced a profound thing: When I shut up, God shows up. Consequently, at some point in my teaching, I have learned to simply shut my notes, and invite the Presence of Jesus to come and speak to people directly. That is when it gets fun! My heartfelt prayer, therefore, as you end this book, is that you experience God speaking to you personally in some new ways that build your faith. I know it is a bold prayer to pray. And yet, I am having faith for you that God loves you more than you can possibly grasp. I am counting on this God of all comfort and love, to show up for you. I am trusting Jesus that the promised Holy Spirit would come to those of us who ask "and guide you into all truth" (John 16:13).

As we end this book, I invite you try the following things as your own personal "holy experiment" in hearing God's voice. The engineer part of me wants to exhort you to be an open-minded scientist in this laboratory of hearing God's voice. Like any experimenter, your job is to listen, and to test out what you hear. You will need to be as objective as possible, open to new insights, and willing to be surprised at the results. Remember that in real life, if you are seeking to understand a new thing scientifically, you do not give up. Instead, you try again if what you first tested out did not work like you expected. The best part is that you do not need to be an expert or have a clue about what you are doing when you ask God to talk to you. He will find a way to get through to you in ways that will astound you! It really is your turn now.

Your personal "holy experiment" to hear God's voice

1 · Design a God Whispers Plan that fits YOU—and own it!
If you want to hear God whisper more in your life, you need to be intentional.

Think about it this way. My high school friend, Julie, is a fantastic surfer. However, she does not live in Hawaii, she lives in California where the water is cold. Julie and her dad learned to surf together, and they had to practice, practice and practice to get good.

If you wanted to become a surfer, and every bit of surfing was new to you, what would you do? Maybe you would hire a surf coach? Probably you would set aside some days each week and find an easy place for beginner surfers. I am guessing you would invest in buying a surfboard or at least secure a borrowed one. Most likely, you would plan on going regularly for months until you got the hang of it. Above all else, you would never give up surfing just because you fell a few times off your board, right? Get my point?

Please do not make hearing God's voice any less important than learning to surf, play the piano, hit golf balls, win tennis tournaments, become a techie, or use your latest computer software (…the list goes on). Learning to hear God's voice more clearly is much easier than you think, but you must be committed to seeking God. If you do, He promises to take your hand and lead you each step of the way.

2 · Choose a specific time and place to meet with God each week in order to "practice" hearing His voice.

This "practice time" is different from your traditional personal "quiet time" Bible study (which is very important, of course). This is a new time between you and God with the specific purpose of practicing hearing His voice. Preferably, this is an extended period of time, a whole day if possible. If you are not experienced in hearing God speak, I would say the longer the better. Still, God gets that you have reality to deal with—crying babies, demanding bosses, grocery shopping, making money, and all the other things screaming for your attention. Rest assured that God understands this about you. And yet, seek to be a Mary instead of a Martha. Mary did not get sucked down by the worries of this life, but instead she sat at Jesus' feet, listening (Luke 10:38-42). Set aside time to hear Him.

3 · Create a personal "whisper bag" and take it with you.

Think about the latest new thing you tried to learn and what gear you needed.

My son's basketball bag is filled with his uniform, shoes, basketball and water bottle. My daughter's swim bag has her swimsuit, shampoos, and goggles. When you seek God, thoughtfully consider what things we have discussed in this book might help you in your journey to hear Him.

Some people find it helpful to have a "whisper bag" in their car at all times with things I mentioned previously: a Bible, pen, journal, worship music, ear phones, iPod, devotional book. One missionary I know always kept a flashlight in his bag because he never knew if the electricity would be on at night in order to see his Bible. Another CEO of a company in the Bay area confessed to me that she stashed a Diet Coke or Red Bull in her bag because she did not want to fall asleep during her time with God! (As an aside: One of the most holy things you can do sometimes is sleep. Remember Elijah? God is OK with you falling asleep if you are that tired.) The rule about the "whisper bag" is to stock it with what works for you! You want to be as prepared as possible when you have that time with your Lord.

4 · Invite Jesus, by the Holy Spirit, to come speak with you.

When you are settled in your selected spot, take some deep breaths and relax. Put on your worship music or just enjoy the quiet if you prefer. Then, in your own words, invite Jesus to come and speak directly to you in a way that you understand. Say, write, or pray it—but just start with the invitation. I typically write a letter to Jesus to get started that goes something like, "Dear Jesus, here I am. I am desperate to hear you. Come and clear the fog and speak to me." I find journaling helps me to focus my wandering mind and clears my head of all distractions.

5 · Listen to some worship music that is meaningful to you.

If you are at a special spot, such as a garden, you might find a private place to sit and worship. For those of you who do not enjoy worship music, do what clears your mind and helps you focus on God: walk on the beach, hike in the woods. Do what works for you and brings you into the Presence of Jesus in a way that moves you.

6 · Ask God to lead you to a specific Bible passage to read.

Ask God to direct you to a specific passage of the Bible to read for today. Close your eyes and listen. God might surprise you when, all of a sudden, a specific Bible verse pops into your head. Go with it. A business executive confessed to me recently that the company had a huge decision to make. Anxious and overwhelmed with fear of making a mistake, the team had asked dozens of people for advice. Still, the answer to the situation was not clear. In a moment of desperation, this man fell to his knees and exclaimed,

"God I don't know what to do in this situation! Help! I know I'm not very good at asking for your help or praying, but if you can, please let me know what to do!" He told me later, "In that very moment, the answer literally came clear in my mind. I was stunned. Could it be God?"

I love that story because it is a great picture of what it is like when people first start seeking God about the stuff that is weighing on their hearts. They take that risky step of praying, and then they are completely caught off guard when God really answers!

Very often, it is a quiet whisper. Do not over-analyze and think, *Could this really be God speaking to ME?* If God whispers a Bible verse into your mind, do not start a mini debate in your mind thinking, *Is this verse really God whispering to me, or perhaps it's just the verse that I heard in some Bible study recently?* Instead, just open your Bible, and turn to that passage. See if it means something to you. You might be surprised. If you do not "hear" any Bible verse, do not sweat it. Open to a passage of the Bible that you want to read. If you are new to reading the Bible, you might try a passage in the New Testament such as in Luke, John, or Romans. If you are struggling with depression, you might consider reading the Psalms.

7 · Invite the Holy Spirit to speak to your heart.

Talk to Jesus about the thing (or things) in your life that you most long to hear His voice about. Tell him your feelings about what is going on, and ask for His wisdom. Try praying the following prayer. (There is nothing magical about the prayer itself, by the way. It is not a formula. Use it if it helps you or just talk to God in your own words.)

Lord, I want to hear your voice speaking to me. Holy Spirit, I invite you into this moment and ask that you would remove any distractions or barriers so I can hear you more clearly. Put over my head the helmet of salvation so that I might have the mind of Christ. In Jesus' name, I forbid the Enemy from speaking to my mind. May the words, impressions, pictures, or senses I get as I pray now be only from you. Help me to grow closer to you through these times of seeking you. Jesus, would you speak to me about _____. Show me your heart and what you want me to see. In Jesus' name, Amen.

8 · Listen for God's still, small voice.

This is the hardest part for most people. In our culture, we have become very good at talking to God but not very good at listening. Here is how I would invite you to think about your connection to God: Pretend you are in a remote part of the jungle in the Congo, calling your best friend at home. The connection is very weak, so you have to listen carefully. You realize it is like tuning into those old radios where the signals are not always great and you have to do some fine tuning to get it work. It takes some tapping into the radio wave.

Similarly, when you are beginning to hear the Holy Spirit in your life, remember it is not a one-way conversation where you immediately pick up a perfectly-clear voice on the other end of the line. Talk to God. Then, take at least two or three minutes of silence and listen for God's voice. Do not worry if your mind wanders or you do not seem to hear anything. This process takes a little practice.

Understand that when God speaks to you, it is not going to be a big, booming voice, but the quiet whisper, the still, small voice. Over time, you will learn to tune into that quiet whisper of God. Be ready, though, for any new impressions, feelings, pictures, or words that pop into your mind. If you do this over time, those things will come. When they do, write them down. The Bible exhorts us not to "...despise the day of small things" (Zechariah 4:10), and this is your time of small beginnings.

9 · Test any whispers you hear that might be from God.

Remember that this is new for most people, and the only way you are going to learn if it is God speaking is to take some risks and ask people. Most of the whispers I hear on the Whisper Scale are at a level two on a scale to 10! I have just learned to step out in faith, with humility, and check them out. Use the guidelines we discussed in chapter nine for how to discern God's voice from your own voice and the Enemy's lies. If it is a word for yourself, share it with people of God you trust. If it is a word for someone else, check out those guidelines in Chapter nine. It is very important to filter what you are hearing through these lenses, for when you do, you will most likely discover that God is speaking to you way more than you thought.

10 · Record in your journal times you thought God might have whispered, and it turned out you were right.
Wow! It really was God! Those times are important to record, because it will build your faith as you keep seeking to hear the Lord speak.

Your small group "holy experiment" in hearing God
Without question, you will grow faster in hearing God's voice if you do these things in community. Think about it like a team sport. If you want to get good at basketball, you can shoot hoops by yourself. However, you are going to really learn to play the game when you join a team. If you cannot find such a group, pray about starting one. If you do, here are some guidelines to create a safe small group to hear God's voice more in your own life and for others:

1 · Choose a weekly meeting time and place.
While it is possible to meet less often, I find that individuals make the most progress in hearing God if they are meeting each week.

2 · Consider reading this book together and having a group discussion.
At the end of the chapters, the "God, please whisper to me now" sections are designed to open up honest conversation. It is really important to remember that everyone will hear differently, so the group leader needs to remind the group often that this is a safe place to try. Encourage those who do not feel they are hearing God as much as others. It will be their turn if they keep at it.

3 · After discussing a chapter, take 30 minutes to pray for each other.
You might break up the time by playing some worship music, or have a group member read a passage of the Bible. Definitely set aside at least 30 minutes for prayer.

4 · Ask for a volunteer "guinea pig."
Ask for a volunteer to be prayed over in order to allow the group members to practice hearing God. You likely will not have time for more than two people per week, unless your group agrees to go longer than an hour. Be sure that people feel freedom to leave on time if they need to and that there are leaders who are willing to stay behind if the ministry time goes long.

5 · Let the "guinea pig" share his or her need. Encourage brevity.
There is a tendency to talk more and pray less. Encourage the person to share briefly what the need is. Sometimes we say, "If Jesus was here now, which we know He is present through the Holy Spirit, what would you ask God to do for you?" That prayer can focus the person more clearly on their felt need.

6 · The group leader should invite the Holy Spirit to come and lead the prayer time.
Pray for the specific need that the volunteer asked the group to pray about. *This is very important!* Even if your group members have other pictures, impressions, or words that they sense that are not related to the person's expressed need for prayer, it is very important that you honor the original prayer request.

7 · Bless the person with peace!
It takes guts to let people pray for you, so always start by praying a blessing of God's peace and love upon the one who volunteered.

8 · Allow a time of quiet listening.
Allow five minutes at least, which will seem long to some. But do not be afraid to wait and be quiet. Then the group should be free to pray as they feel led. Get comfortable with silence.

9 · Push the pause button!

Stop the prayer time intermittently. Ask the person if he or she is hearing, sensing, or seeing anything that might be God speaking to them. Next, ask the group members to share if they are seeing, sensing, or hearing anything that might be from God. Again, the main thing is to create a safe community to try, and if you share everything in love with humility, that trying means sometimes you will get it wrong. That is not failure! Getting things wrong is how you learn. Use the guidelines for sharing words found in Chapter 10, on "How to encourage hearing God's voice without blowing up your church."

10 · Thank God for any specific words and continue praying.

If you are not hearing anything specific, do not be concerned. Keep asking God, like the persistent widow in Scripture.

11 · Give everyone a chance to share the area of life where each longs to hear God whisper.

This should not take a long time. However, it is important for the group to be praying for one another during the week about the specific areas for individuals where they are asking God to speak.

What do you still need?

After trying your individual and small group "holy experiments" in hearing God speak, what do you still need? Hearing God's voice is a not a quick process, it is a life-long journey. If you persevere in the journey, you are likely to have these things happen to you at some point: One, you will have some amazing encounters with the Living God that will build your faith. Two, you will have moments of frustration and disappointment. We are not with Jesus, yet, in Heaven where we are seeing "face to face." One promise I feel comfortable making to you is this: If you press on in seeking to hear Jesus more in your life, God will find His way to get through to you. He has promised that He will "never leave you nor forsake you" (Deuteronomy 31:8).

As you travel on this journey, you may have questions and need encouragement along the way. I would encourage you to seek help in many directions! Ask your pastor for wisdom. Seek out conferences where hearing God speak is a normal part of the Christian life. I welcome you to visit us at www.christypierce. org On the website, you will find small group materials with resources to start your own group. You will also see opportunities to attend one of our whispers conferences. Finally, we offer some online coaching to troubleshoot the issues that come up for you or your church as you seek to follow God and hear His voice more. We are here to help you in your journey and be your cheerleaders as you follow the Holy Spirit in hearing God more.

Do not give up

One time I was doing a conference and a lovely lady, I will call her Jenny, came up to me after I finished speaking. Her face looked sad, and I could tell she was hesitant to tell me why. I asked what was wrong and if I could pray for her. With tears streaming down her face, she finally blurted out,

"Christy, I came to this conference hoping I'd hear God speak to me, and I tried hard. My marriage is very rocky, and I really wanted God to tell me what to do. I asked God to talk to me, and I feel like a failure." She took a deep breath and said, emotion filling her eyes, "It seemed like everyone else here had this great God-whispering experience, and I was the only one who heard nothing." My heart sank. I was so very grateful that she was courageous enough to come and vent her frustration at God and at the process.

I did not pretend to have easy answers, but I asked if I could pray for her right then. She shut her eyes, and we prayed together. I asked God to break through the fog she was seeing, and to reveal Himself to her. I asked Him to speak about the issue heavy on her heart. As we quietly stood there, I watched as a transformation came over her face. Instead of sadness and tears, a smile broke out on her face. She looked up at me, and said,

"Christy, I've never had this happen before, but I see this very faint picture of myself dressed in white, and God standing there beside me. I don't know what it means, but I feel a peace washing over me that I know isn't me—it's God!" I have keep in touch with Jenny, and honestly, her circumstances have not changed much in her marriage. But she claims that since that day, her relationship with Jesus has been more real, deeper, and has become the source that keeps her going.

My eyes seek out those people in the audience who, like Jenny, may not be hearing God. Not everyone hears God right away and there are reasons, as we discussed in the chapter on earplugs, that we might be blocked from hearing God's voice at certain times in our lives. That feeling of disconnect is hard, and in those times, God wants to whisper to us most of all. Let us, then, rise up and encourage one another. As some read this book, I know many will have these incredible mountaintop moments where they hear God speak to in new ways, and I thank God and celebrate those life-changing experiences.

At the same time, I am aware that hearing God is a life-long journey, and there are times, where we pray just as hard, just as fervently, and hear nothing. If that is your experience, I want to encourage you that this does not mean God loves you less, or you are less gifted, or because of your sin, or that you will never have experiences of hearing God speak that minister to your soul deeply. Please do not give up. Whatever your experience has been reading this book, or trying the "holy experiments," please do not throw in the towel because you did not hear things that other people did. Here is what you do: Pray again. Keep at it. Do not give up. Get help.

Conclusion: You can do it!

A man had been walking many months through a dry, barren land. Thirsty and weary from the long journey, he came to the edge of a cliff where a chasm separated him from vibrant land filled with sparkling waterfalls and rivers. He longed to reach that land so he could drink deeply from those waters and rest his tired body in the green grass under the trees. But the chasm that lay between looked too steep, and he feared it was too big of a leap to get from where he was to the new land. Suddenly, an angel behind him whispered,

"Do not be afraid! It's not that big of a leap! Take my hand and I'll lead you to the bridge which you can cross, one step at a time, into the Promised Land you long to reach." The angel took the man's hand, and led him to a long bridge that connected where he was to the new land, glistening in the distant horizon. Waiting at the bridge was Jesus, smiling at the man, saying,

"Take my hand. I'll show you the way, and I will not let you fall." Step by step, the man crossed holding Jesus' hand. Finally, with joy, he made it to the land flowing with milk and honey, by taking one step at a time.

This story is a good illustration of the spiritual journey to hear God's voice more in our lives. As we come to the end of this book, I invite you to picture yourself in the story above. Where are you? Are you at the edge of the cliff, looking beyond what you are currently experiencing of God, fearful that you will not ever hear God's voice more in a way that is real for you? Does it feel like this hearing God stuff might be possible for other people, but like too big of a leap for you? Can you picture yourself, taking all the good things of God you have learned so far in your life, and still cross into a "new land" of the Spirit where you hear God more clearly whispering to you in your daily life?

If you are like many people I encounter, you might long to hear God more in your life, but it seems like too big a leap to get there. May I please end this book by reassuring you, no matter how far away you feel from God, that it is not too big of a leap in your spiritual journey. You can be yourself, with all the good things you have known of God so far in your life, and you can add to that a whole new experiential prayer life where you hear God whispering about the big things that matter to you. It is possible because it is God's deep desire for you. Do not believe the Enemy's lie that this "hearing God stuff" is for other people and just will not happen for you. Do not let the Liar do that to you.

If you keeping asking God to turn up the volume, He will do it. When my son, Benji, was just learning to walk, he would stand up, and take those little baby steps so fitting for his age. It was my greatest joy, as his parent, to stand beside him and hold his hand, saying,

"You can do it Benj! That's it! One step at a time, Benji Bo!" As he was learning to walk, I got to hold his hand, help him up if he fell, and make sure he did not get hurt along the way. That same baby boy is now a very strong runner.

Jesus has your hand. Wherever you are on your own spiritual journey, He wants you to know that the leap to more of His whispering voice is not too big for you. He will take you to the bridge and help you cross over. He will not let you fall, for if you put your hope in Him, His promise is hope never disappoints (Romans 5:5). He is the Good Parent, who will be beside you each step of the way, helping you grow up into the person of God He created who can experience a deep, intimate relationship with Him. You can hear His voice behind you each step of the way, saying, *This is the way, walk in it* (Isaiah 30:21). May the Lord bless you, and open your ears and eyes, and do what only He can do: speak to you in ways that are exceeding above all that you have asked or imagined.

Amen.

Made in the USA
San Bernardino, CA
27 March 2016